# My Next Move

## Positioning Yourself to Win
## the Game of Life

Nichole Cornelius

ISBN: 0692372881
ISBN-13: 978-0692372883

# DEDICATION

To my Storyline tribe of creators—Amy, Joe, Kathreen, Mary, and Molly—this book is for you. I took a risk to be a creator and not a consumer. My hope is that this book inspires you to share your story and your creation. The world needs your stories. The world needs you.

*Stones in the road? I save every single one, and one day I'll build a castle.*—Fernando Pessoa

# CONTENTS

## Phase One: The Chess Opening

## Phase Two: The Middle Game

## Phase Three: The End Game

# ACKNOWLEDGMENTS

There are so many people that have walked alongside me on this journey from brokenness to wholeness and I cannot count them all. Some have been key players in my life often carrying me through some very dark and difficult moments, and others have simply held my hand and offered words of encouragement to guide me along the way. I am grateful to each and every one of you. You have made me a better person.

In addition to all these wonderful people, I would personally like to thank a few more who positively altered the course of direction in my life.

To my former pastor Denny Livingston—Throughout the years under your leadership, you confirmed the concept and details of this book time and time again. Your words, your teachings, and your insight led me to healing. I will be eternally grateful.

To my friend Rob—You were an unexpected surprise. You caught me off guard and unnerved me. Before we met, my writing was stale and lifeless. You helped me find my voice and bring my words to life. I became a better writer because of you.

To my cousin Shelly, my first friend and my partner in crime—I was your little shadow, mimicking your every move. I relied on you and trusted you to lead me in life. As I grew up and developed confidence in myself and my ability, I was able to find my own way. Through it all, you never left my side. Thank you for supporting me, encouraging me, and calling and scheduling all my haircut appointments throughout the years <insert smiley face>.

To my precious Matt, the one who gets me and who speaks my language—Words could never fully describe how I feel about you. All I know for sure is that you showed up in my life at exactly the right place and time. Through your love and support, I found the courage to believe in myself and live out the person I was created to "be." Thank you for shared dreams, laughter, and the vision and inspiration for Bookends Media. You and I share the same heartbeat, and together we are going to do amazing things.

Above all else, I would like to thank God for loving me, guiding me, teaching me, correcting me, protecting me, and being my constant companion along this journey. I hope my words paint a true depiction of who You are. You are a God of grace, hope, and love. Let my faith and story be a testament to You.

# FORWARD

## By Shelly Deason

When I started blogging in 2008, I did not consider the impact it would have on any life other than my own. As the stories of my past unfolded, good and bad, I had people approach me with their own stories and pain. When my cousin Nichole came to me and let me know that my blog had given her the courage to open up the old wounds and situations of our childhood, it made me realize our words can be a balm to those who are struggling.

She decided to start sharing her story and let God lead her into whatever direction He chose. From her journey and blog this passion for writing was birthed, and the scripture of Isaiah 61:3 has truly been fulfilled in her life.

*....to give unto them beauty for ashes, the oil of joy for mourning, the garment of praise for the spirit of heaviness; that they might be called trees of righteousness, the planting of the LORD, that he might be glorified.*

Many people with traumatic childhoods are not able to heal and become productive and healthy individuals because it is easier to stuff down the pain and let that pain destroy you instead of using it to minister to others. Nichole bears her heart and lets us know that while our lives might not be ideal by any means, God still has a plan if we follow His lead.

Much of our lives are spent realizing that God has different plans for us than we have for ourselves. Sometimes we struggle with those plans and God has us linger there in our sorrow. When we realize what we are to learn from the situation, we get to make our next move towards freedom.

Nichole has found that freedom and it shines forth through these pages to give hope to the reader, letting them know that no matter what, God always knows what our next move needs to be. It is such an honor to write this forward and to be a part of her story. I hope you feel the same.

.

# INTRODUCTION

*I am on a journey with my work, my explorations, and a few sad stories. I travel with a suitcase full of outrageous blessings. I am on a quest for truth, beauty, and quiet joy. I am an artist, a writer, and an explorer.*—Unknown

I first began writing and pursuing the art of writing passionately in 2009 when I created my blog *The Journey to Finish the Race.* The blog was founded on the scripture Philippians 3:13-14—"forgetting those things behind and pressing forward ahead."

I settled on this scripture and used it as a foundation for my writing so I could constantly be reminded to focus on living in the possibilities of the here and now instead of the shadows of what was clearly behind me. I spent the majority of my life chasing what was taken from me instead of pursuing what was given. It was time for a change.

The blog served as my virtual journal capturing the attempts to move forward, the setbacks, and what I learned in the process, but it also was a means to pull me out of hiding. I always lived a life in the shadows and tried my best to

1

remain hidden. It's a defense mechanism—let no one in, don't get hurt. However, this blog began tearing down the walls I created and led me towards the path of vulnerability. I felt safe behind my computer screen. I could share my thoughts freely with no fear of rejection or judgment.

As I began to find my voice and my platform, I began to blossom as a writer. I found writing to be very therapeutic. As buried feelings and emotions surfaced and transformed to words on a page, the pain that once had a choke hold on me, began to loosen its grip.

Over time, my words began to travel to the hearts of others, and I began to build a readership. It turned out that my writing had a therapeutic impact on my readers as well. Friends and even strangers would email thanking me for saying the things they didn't have the courage to say. It was actually during this time in my life that I fell in love with writing and realized the weight it carried for my purpose in life.

My new love for writing turned into a desire to write a book. I have always wanted to write a book, but I could never come up with a concept or find the guts to pursue this dream. That all changed five years ago when I started the transformation of turning my blog into a book. This book spans the last 39 years of my life, and the creation of the book was a journey in itself. The book has taken many different shapes and forms over the last five years until I finally settled on my concept in 2010—the game of chess.

I made countless edits and revisions before I finally felt that all the pages came together. It seemed I had a few more chapters to live out before the book could finally come to a close. This is very much like the story of my life—countless re-writes until my life finally came together and I found my purpose.

*Do not go where the path may lead, go instead where there is no path and leave a trail.*—Ralph Waldo Emerson

On the eve of New Year's Eve 2014, a classmate and friend passed away due to complications of cardiac arrest. He was only 39 years old. He was a talented musician, he loved and served the Lord, and he was devoted to his wife and two beautiful daughters. His death was a tragic and unexpected loss.

Thousands of friends, classmates, family, and members of our community poured into the church which held his funeral. His funeral was one of the most moving services I have ever attended. It's almost indescribable. It was a true celebration of his life. Stories were shared, tears were shed, and songs were sung all celebrating the short time he spent on earth.

As the service was coming to a close, my dear friend Ann-Marie leaned over to me and said, "Nick, when I leave this world, will I be remembered like him? Everybody loved Ty. I want to be remembered for something. I want to leave a mark on the world just like he did." I squeezed her hand in agreement and just let my tears fall.

I read this particular passage in *Scary Close*, the latest book by Donald Miller, and it made me realize what kind of impression I want to leave.

*I have no idea why one person can be handed a tragic past and become healthy and selfless while another amplifies their pain into the lives of others. Almost without exception, the most beautiful, selfless people I've met are ones who've experienced personal tragedy. They remind me of the trees I occasionally stumble across in the Columbia River Gorge, the ones that got started under boulders and wound slowly around the rock face to find an alternative route to the sun.*

I love trees, especially the ones that Donald Miller described. I like to spend my free time hiking in the woods in various parks in Nashville, Tennessee. As I make my way through the hike, I pause to look at the various trees and their roots. The deeply knotted roots, so tightly threaded into the ground, anchor down the trees and allow the trees to withstand the elements of life—wind, rain, snow, and ice. Without those roots grasping so tightly to the ground, the trees would not last. They would collapse from the weight of the surrounding environment.

Donald Miller states that he has no idea why one person can be given a tragic past and become a healthy and selfless individual while another can project their pain on another. I have an idea and it is evident in my own life. I am like the tree Donald Miller described. I had a rough start, but through perseverance and determination, I found an alternate path around that troubled start and positioned myself to live a healthy and successful life.

I know that without a shadow of a doubt, if I was not grounded in the Lord, I would have become the one projecting my pain on others instead of inspiring and helping others live out a better story. For without my faith, my belief in God, and my reliance on Him, I would not be standing here today. I would have collapsed a long time ago. I am grateful for the roots that have sustained me. I am most grateful for grace.

As I think back to the day my friends and I had to say good-bye to our friend, although the day was hard, it was a joyous occasion too. After the service, we went out for dinner and sat around the table sharing stories and laughter. My friend Julie brought her yearbooks so we could take a walk down memory lane. For that brief moment in time, we focused on all the memories we shared and left feeling inspired to live a better story.

For the next 100 plus pages, you get to take a walk with me down memory lane. As you turn the pages, you will experience the highs and the lows of my life. There are a few painful chapters to walk through, but they were all instrumental in fulfilling my purpose. There are even a few mishaps which hopefully will provide you a few laughs.

You may not agree with everything I say. You may also think I share too much or not enough at all. I don't claim to be an expert on life, but I have found a path that has lead me to a very fulfilling and blessed life. I have lived out every ounce of these pages, and there are a few pages I would like to tear out completely. What matters most to me is for once, I completely own my story, and I am not ashamed to share it. Thank you from the bottom of my heart for taking a chance on me and my book. I hope by sharing my story and my heart, you are able to realize your place in this world and are inspired to leave your own legacy just like my friend Ty did for his community and his own little world.

*You cannot get through one single day without having an impact on the world around you. What you do makes a difference, and you have to decide what kind of difference you want to make.*—Jane Goodall.

## The Oak Tree

A mighty wind blew night and day.
It stole the oak tree's leaves away.
Then snapped its boughs and pulled its bark
Until the oak was tired and stark.
But still the oak tree held its ground,
While other trees fell all around.
The weary wind gave up and spoke,
"How can you still be standing, Oak?"
The oak tree said, "I know that you can break
Each branch of mine in two, carry every leaf away,
Shake my limbs, and make me sway.
But I have roots stretched in the earth,
Growing stronger since my birth.
You'll never touch them, for you see,
They are the deepest part of me.
Until today, I wasn't sure
Of just how much I could endure.
But now I've found, with thanks to you,
I'm stronger than I ever knew."

— Johnny Ray Ryder Jr.

# 1 THE GAME OF LIFE

*When it comes to the game of life, I figure I've played the whole course.*—Lee Trevino

Long before the days of playing Frogger, Ms. Pacman, and Donkey Kong J.R. on the Atari 2600, I spent most of my free time playing board games. My family and I lived for playing games. We played every game Milton Bradley and Parker Brothers ever created. We played Sorry, Aggravation, Battleship, Monopoly, and Life. In my household, board games were as sacred as milk, bread, and my beloved Kool-Aid. If a game was created, my family was playing it.

On Saturday mornings, my cousins, Troy and David, and I could be found sprawled out on my grandma's living room floor playing board games. I remember these days as if they were yesterday; our heads were propped up by our hands and elbows, and our feet were kicking aimlessly in the air. The fibers of the living room carpet, worn thin from years of traffic, felt like a Brillo pad brushing up against my skin and left its mark of irritation.

The smells of Saturday morning breakfast filled the air as

Grandma was away in the kitchen, frying up eggs and bacon and making us pancakes. When breakfast was ready, no amount of effort from Grandma could peel us away from our game, not even her tasty buttermilk pancakes drenched in butter and maple syrup. We didn't care about food; we just wanted to play.

Playing games was our chance to escape the woes of life: fighting with friends, going to school, doing homework, and cleaning our rooms. These were the days we lived for, the glory days of our youth. We were important and we were winners.

We put every ounce of emotion into playing those games. We worked hard to be the wealthiest player at the end of the game by collecting our paychecks and buying up hotels on Park Avenue. We fought over which piece we would be, the Scottish Terrier, the thimble, the red or blue piece, and who would go first.

We taunted and teased each other over the moves made. We paraded our wins and rejoiced when one of us lost a turn, got sent back to the start, or had to sell a property. Just when I thought I was almost home or inches from winning the game, Troy or David would cry out, "Sorry!" in a very sarcastic tone, which would send me all the way back home.

We desperately wanted to be crowned the winner and not to come in dead last. We celebrated our wins and cried many tears when we lost. The lessons learned playing those games were invaluable. We learned how to get along with one another and how to wait our turn. We learned the consequences of cheating and taking shortcuts. We learned how to lose even if we went out kicking and screaming. Most importantly, we learned how to get right back in the game.

Out of all the games I played, Life was my favorite. The fact that I could cruise around in my pink Cadillac, with my pink and blue twins in tow, up and down the hills of life was fascinating and exciting.

When I came across the fork in the road to either pursue the path of college or an immediate job, I chose whatever path was right at that time. I didn't listen to what others advised me to do. I chose my own path. I was in the driver seat of life, and I liked it that way. It satisfied my craving for control.

The game Life was originally called "The Checkered Game of Life." The game was a modified checkerboard where the player's objective was to land on "good" spaces and collect 100 points. Isn't the goal of life to advance to "good" spaces?

Work hard, get the promotion. Go to the gym, develop a lean body. Fall in love, get married. Every move we make increases the value of our life. We may not collect points, but our lives increase in value by every experience and every person we encounter.

We age, but we never outgrow games. As adults, we play Apples to Apples, Catch Phrase, Words with Friends, and Candy Crush. Games follow us all through life. Although life is not a game, there are similarities. There is always an opponent in pursuit of us, trying to trip us, make us fall, and lead us to defeat.

There are rules to follow, decisions to make, risks to take, and a desire to win and be successful. The heartache, loss, and stress that accompany such choices and experiences in life are not included in the fine print on the back of the box. We have to figure life out for ourselves, and we do that by playing the game.

Life is more than just spinning a wheel or rolling the dice. We don't just land on success, good health, and prosperity— we progress. We take steps forward and backwards. There are even times when we feel as if we are running in circles. We rise and we fall. We succeed and we fail. We hurt and we heal. Sometimes our pieces get knocked over, captured, or sent back to the start, and we have to begin the process all over again.

*Life is a balance of holding on and letting go.*—Rumi

Mark Batterson, author of *The Circle Maker*, said, "There are basically two approaches to life: playing to win and playing not to lose. Too many of us are tentatively playing the game of life as if the purpose is to arrive safely at death." I believe the approach you take is how you value life. As for me, I am playing to win, and I always will take this approach.

I am competitive by nature, and I want to win and win big. I want everything I can possibly dream of. I want the career, to be a published author and travel across the country speaking and sharing my story. I want to be a wife and mother. I want to experience ultimate joy. I simply want to be happy and healthy.

How do you view life? Are you living a full life or are you simply going through the motions? Do you want to fulfill your life's purpose or safely arrive home? Are you going to play the game or sit out on the sidelines? There is a game being played whether you have an active role or not. I hope by reading my story you feel inspired to take charge of your life and actively play the game, and most importantly, you play to win.

*Take what comes your way as an opportunity and not a burden. There is always a plan. Sometimes it takes a little longer to understand the journey of life, but in the end everything is meant to be.*—Kellin Quinn

# 2 THE GAME MAKER

*I am convinced, the way one plays chess always reflects the player's personality. If something defines his character, then it will also define his way of playing.* —Vladimir Kramnik

Mark Batterson said, "Every book has a backstory. There is a moment when an idea is conceived in the imagination of an author, and this idea is destined to be a book." This moment happened for me in February 2010 when I began drafting a blog titled *A Game of Chess*.

My knowledge of chess was limited. I had never fully researched, studied, or even played the game. The only game I had ever played that closely resembled chess was checkers, which really is not a good comparison.

Chess is complex. There are many pieces involved, and each one has a specific rule of movement it must follow. As a result, I found myself with writer's block. For some strange reason, I felt a strong connection to the game and abandoned the draft in hopes of completing it one day.

The reason for this abandoned blog finally surfaced in May 2011 and everything began to tie together. One Saturday evening I was attending the church Point of Mercy's fourth-anniversary service and Pastor Bobby McCool was invited to preach. Pastor Bobby McCool was the cousin of Point of Mercy's pastor Denny Livingston. The title of his message was "The Art of Positioning." His message focused on the struggles and the opposition Point of Mercy faced, and how the church was in a period of rebuilding and growth.

Pastor Bobby McCool shared the story of Moses and the Israelites, God's chosen people, and how they were instructed to build God's Tabernacle exactly in the pattern He showed them. The blueprint for the Tabernacle was very detailed as found in Exodus 25 and 26. The plans were so detailed that it spanned 37 verses as partially captured below.

*Have the people make an Ark of acacia wood—a sacred chest 45 inches long, 27 inches wide, and 27 inches high. Overlay it inside and outside with pure gold, and run a molding of gold all around it.* Exodus 25: 10–11 (NLT)

*Then make a table of acacia wood, 36 inches long, 18 inches wide, and 27 inches high. Overlay it with pure gold and run a gold molding around the edge.* Exodus 25: 23–24 (NLT)

*Make a lampstand of pure, hammered gold. Make the entire lampstand and its decorations of one piece—the base, center stem, lamp cups, buds, and petals. Make it with six branches going out from the center stem, three on each side.* Exodus 25: 31–32 (NLT)

*Make the Tabernacle from ten curtains of finely woven linen. Decorate the curtains with blue, purple, and scarlet thread and with skillfully embroidered cherubim.* Exodus 26: 1 (NLT)

*For the framework of the Tabernacle, construct frames of acacia wood. Each frame must be 15 feet high and 27 inches wide, with two pegs under each frame. Make all the frames identical.* Exodus 26: 15–17 (NLT)

Once the Tabernacle was built specifically as instructed, God's presence would appear in the form of a cloud. His presence was thick and draped over his people as a means to protect them. The cloud also served as a guide to lead them to their next destination. Any time the cloud stopped, they stopped. Any time the cloud moved, they moved.

God accompanied the Israelites every step of the way as they made way to their final destination, the Promised Land (Genesis 28:15). The Promised Land was the land given to the Israelites by God. This was the land of prosperity, or the land of milk and honey as the Bible describes it.

Point of Mercy had endured many obstacles in the church's existence. Point of Mercy was led by many pastors up until Pastor Denny Livingston became lead pastor. When he took over, there were only seven members remaining. He took the remaining members and together they slowly started building the church from the ground up. Restoring the broken relationships with the existing members set the foundation for the Tabernacle. At that point, the church began to grow and began creating the Tabernacle.

As Moses, the Israelites, and Point of Mercy have had to build the Tabernacle before God would appear, we have the same blueprint on our lives. Our lives are the building of the Tabernacle. With every step, every experience, and every person we encounter, we are building a house for God. Every aspect of our life has to be positioned according to God's plan in order for Him to "show up" in our lives.

Every person we encounter, every position we find ourselves in, whether it be our job or at home, has a purpose. We are aligned for specific purposes. God lines us up in positions to cross paths with people who influence and change us. He lines us up with experiences, both positive and negative, to challenge us, test us, and make us grow. Through these encounters and experiences, God is transforming us and positioning us to fulfill His purpose created for our lives.

Mark Batterson described positioning as this, "Like a grandmaster who strategically positions chess pieces on a chessboard, God is always preparing us and positioning us for divine appointments." I envision God sitting at an overly large and sturdy wooden table, in His oversized chair playing chess.

The chessboard, strong and durable like God himself, is crafted with alternating black and white squares. His elbow is planted firmly on the table and serves to prop up His head. He carefully studies each and every possible move. One by one, He makes moves in our lives. He is orchestrating the events in our life by the movement of the pieces.

As God contemplates which move to make, I hear him saying, *Yes, that move looks nice. That will open up a whole lot of opportunity for Nichole. Oh yes, I'll allow that move. Nichole will be better and stronger for it. Oh no, I have to block that move. I see danger up ahead. I'll send her this way instead.*

God has an aerial view, an advantage that we do not have. He can see what lies ahead and what trouble we may encounter. Therefore, He may interject and block a move, or He may allow it altogether. He may send you down a completely different path than the one you had envisioned. What seems like a derailment may be His plan all along. All you have to do is trust Him, which is easier said than done.

*God is strategically orchestrating your steps. Rest in knowing that nothing happens unless it moves you toward your destiny.*—Joel Osteen

Summers in Tennessee are typically scorching hot and the air is sticky. On this particular Sunday afternoon in August 2012, the weather was unexpectedly fall like. The air was crisp and refreshing to consume. I took full advantage of the pleasant surprise and went for a hike at Percy Warner Park. Others must have received the same invitation because the trail was packed with people. Some people were traveling alone with their music, and some were traveling with two-legged, as well as four-legged, friends.

The landscape was visually appealing. The trees were lush showing signs of life and spilled out of their boundaries into the trail, making the path very narrow.

Warner Woods Trail 2.5 Loop, Percy Warner Park

About half way through my 2.5- mile hike, I came across a dad and his two young children who had stopped to look at a squirrel running up a tree. The father appeared middle-aged, the girl was around eight, and the boy about five. I overheard the girl ask, "Dad, who put the acorns on the trees?" As she asked the question, I felt myself wanting to pause and wait for his answer. I wasn't trying to intrude or invade their privacy, but I got caught up in their moment of family bonding.

For most of my life, my dad has been absent more than he has been present. My dad was more like a part-time dad, only around on the weekends. I longed for a fatherly connection, and I longed for days spent hiking in a park and having casual yet meaningful conversations about acorns in trees.

Instead of staying to hear the answer, I greeted them and went on my way. In looking back, I wonder what the father's answer had been. Would he answer with science or would he credit God for creating the acorns?

In my own life, I have had many, many questions about why things have happened the way they did. I have received answers to only some. Not having answers to some of life's most painful questions has caused me a great deal of pain, but somehow I managed to move on.

My mom gave me this poem "The Father and the Child" by Nancy Romaine, many, many years ago. For some reason, it gave me a sense of peace, so I kept it framed as a reminder of the journey.

### *The Father and the Child*
The Father spoke:
Come, child, let us journey together.
*Where shall we go, Father?*
To a distant land, another kingdom.
*So the journey will be long?*
Yes, we must travel every day.
*When will we reach our destination?*
At the end of your days.
*And who will accompany us?*
Joy and Sorrow.
*Must Sorrow travel with us?*
Yes, she is necessary to keep you close to Me.

*But I want only Joy.*
It's only with Sorrow that you will know true Joy.
*What must I bring?*
A willing heart to follow Me.
*What shall I do on the journey?*
There is only one thing that you must do—
Stay close to Me. Let nothing distract you.
Always keep your eyes on Me.
*And what will I see?*
You will see My glory.
*And what will I know?*
You will know My heart.
The Father stretched out His hand.
The child, knowing the great love her Father had for her, placed her hand in His and began her journey.
—Nancy Romaine

Just as this poem suggests, the journey is going to be filled with both joy and sorrow, and sorrow is what keeps us close to God. For without sorrow, we would not need Him. The road to my place of promise has been long and laborious, and the surface has not always been smooth. There were parts of the path that were completely paved with sorrow, but joy managed to peek its head through the cracks. I had grown weary and frustrated, and at times I lost the desire to go on. However, I trusted God, and I had a willing heart to go on with the journey.

My niece Madison in Gatlinburg with her dad

As I look at this picture of my niece Madison riding on the shoulders of her dad, I am reminded that even though the journey can be long and tiresome, God will be with us every step of the way. He will fulfill the role of the absentee parent. He will pick us up and carry us when we are tired. He will stay the course until He has delivered on all His promises. All we have to do is trust Him and hang on for the ride.

The Lord never meant to settle in one place and neither should we. We were meant to keep moving from one place to the next until we reach our place of promise whether that is completion, restoration, healing, freedom, or love. Even there, we will still have more obstacles to face and hurdles to climb. We will never stop growing, maturing, and moving forward until the day Jesus returns (Philippians 1:6).

I hope that by the time you reach the end of the book, you will see why you have been placed in the positions you have been. You will be tested, tried, and proved. You will be knocked down, sidetracked, and might find yourself starting over. Hopefully, you will see why you have had to journey through these positions, either God allowed or ordered, to reach your place of promise. I hope you continue on with me to *my next move*.

*It is good to have an end to journey toward; but it is the journey that matters in the end.*—Ernest Hemingway

# 3 THE DESIGN OF THE GAME

*If life doesn't offer a game worth playing, then invent a new one.*—
Anthony J. D'Angelo

Every detail of chess is vital, right down to the board it is played on. The board is designed with a checkerboard pattern, which consists of 64 squares alternating in color from dark to light. To facilitate the moves, all squares are given a name. A square is named by the combination of its column-letter and row-number, e.g., the square in the lower-left corner (for white) is a1. The columns are named, from left to right, a, b, c, d, e, f, g, h. The rows are numbered 1, 2, 3, 4, 5, 6, 7, 8; the lowest row has number 1, and the upper-most row has number 8.

There is a design for the game, and I believe there is a design for our life. Our lives follow a specific pattern, individually tailored to meet God's design and His purpose (Jeremiah 1:5). Donald Miller, author of *A Million Miles in a Thousand Years*, said, "Life itself may be designed to change us so that we evolve from one kind of person to another. We are designed to live through something rather than attain something and the thing we were meant to live through was designed to change us."

The thing we were meant to live through, whether it is abuse, loss, or sickness, differs greatly from one person to the next. In order to live out the design for our lives, we have to accept every event, even the ones that we would rather not encounter.

*For I know the plans I have for you, declares the Lord, plans to prosper you and not to harm you, plans to give you hope and a future.—* Jeremiah 29:11 (NIV)

In elementary school, I use to play M.A.S.H (Mansion Apartment Shack House) with my friends. We played to predict our future—our spouse, the number of kids we would have, the kind of car we would drive, and the kind of house we would live in.

The game starts by you writing out MASH at the top of your paper. Then, you make a list of three names or things to fit into the categories of kids, cars, and pets.

One person begins drawing out a swirl on the paper, and another yells out, "Stop." The number of lines in the swirl indicates what word you land on and have to cross off throughout the process of elimination. This continues until you are left with a mansion, a Cadillac, two kids, and a husband named Kirk Cameron. At least, that was the plan for my life <insert smiley face>.

No matter how many swirls end up on the page and what words remain, life does not always turn out as predicted. Mine did not. There are some big question marks still circling above my head. For instance, why am I not married yet? Why have I not had any children yet? Why have I not caught my big break yet? The only thing that brings me peace in the mystery is knowing God is holding out for something better. *Not yet, Nichole. Wait, I have something better planned for you. I have a plan.*

I believe we would relieve ourselves of so many unnecessary heartbreaks and pressures if we would stop planning so many details of our lives and just let them unfold naturally. There are reasons we are still single, reasons we cannot or have not had a child, and reasons as to why we have not caught our big break. That piece of our lives has to fit perfectly in the exact spot and at exactly the right time. We have to build the Tabernacle brick by brick and exactly as the design states.

*We must be willing to let go of the life we planned so as to have the life that is waiting for us.*—Joseph Campbell

My cousin Shelly and I spent many weekends with our maternal great-grandmother Memaw Bertha. Memaw Bertha was mean and had a foul mouth, but deeply loved us great-grandkids. She spoiled us with trips to Wal-Mart, McDonald's, and Burglar Chef (Burger Chef), as she called it. Bless her heart, she could not pronounce anything correctly.

After our bellies were full from our happy meal, we would gather around her kitchen table and work jigsaw puzzles. We did not work 50- to 100-piece puzzles either. Memaw worked those large 500- to 1,000-piece puzzles. I am not sure why Memaw chose such challenging puzzles. Maybe the picture of the puzzle was appealing and caught her eye. Maybe she simply liked a challenge. Maybe she liked to get lost in the detail. Whatever the reasons behind her choices, we went along with her plan.

Memaw taught us strategies to work jigsaw puzzles. First, you study the image or design of the puzzle. Next, you pour out the pieces in your work area, sort them by color, and place them into piles. Work the outside edge first and form your foundation. Keep working through the puzzle, feel the shapes, and move the pieces around until you find their proper place.

John Spilsbury created the first jigsaw puzzle in 1767. The concept of the jigsaw puzzle required the assembly of numerous, small, oddly-shaped interlocking pieces. When completed, the puzzle created a complete picture. I read in the article "Jigsaw Puzzle History" that John was a teacher in England and created the puzzle with the purpose of teaching geography. As his students put the pieces together, they would learn how different countries connected to one another.

*If you'll stay in faith, before long, you'll see how every setback, every disappointment was simply another piece of your puzzle.*—Joel Osteen

I see the game of chess like one giant jigsaw puzzle. We have to work through each position, each piece, one at a time, to make the connections. Looking at an individual piece or a position, it is hard to envision how the whole design will come together. As you begin to assemble the puzzle, to be a part of the process, and feel the emotions attached to them, you begin to see how the positions connect to one another, thereby creating the big picture.

As we grow through life, I envision our childhood as the outside edge of the puzzle. As we grow and age, with each experience, another piece is laid, and another, and another until the puzzle is complete. The bigger the vision or purpose for our lives, the more pieces, or positions, we have to work through.

Sometimes the pieces don't seem as if they are going to fit. You twist and turn the pieces, and at times, you try to force them to fit. It's aggravating. *Why won't the piece go in there? I know it fits.* I've been known to jam one piece into another one and leave it hanging there out of place due to frustration. Then, after I settle down, I eventually find where it belongs.

Working jigsaw puzzles was not an overnight job, it took time. Rarely did Memaw, Shelly, and I finish a puzzle in one weekend. Piles of puzzle pieces could be found lying on her kitchen table for a great deal of time. Sometimes, the puzzle was left because it was too challenging. Other times, we had to walk away from it and give our eyes a rest. The remaining pieces to the puzzles would sit in their piles waiting to be used.

I don't think Memaw realized she was teaching us a very important lesson about the process and timing of life. Life is a process. It is like one giant puzzle, and it unfolds and comes together one piece at a time. At times the process is painful and drawn out. It seems as if we will never find where our piece fits. So, we have to sit in our little pile of pieces and wait for God to move and place us in our next position.

*A person can grow only as much as his horizon allows.*—John Powell

I have fallen in love with the TV show *The Amazing Race*. I love the whole concept of the show: partner up with a friend, spouse, or sibling and compete in the race around the world to be crowned the winner. The contestants on Season 19 traveled 40,000 miles across 20 cities and 4 continents to claim victory at the final finish line. The teams take pit stops so they can rest up for the next leg of the race. The team to come in last place in each leg is eliminated.

I love the contestants' spirit and their desire to win. There are setbacks and obstacles to overcome. They have to work closely and efficiently with their teammate which often leads to conflict and tension, which evidently is good for the ratings. How disheartening is it to see the contestants get so close to the million-dollar prize and not win over *one* wrong move?

As I step across the finish line of my own life, I have great fear of hearing Phil Keoghan, the host of the *Amazing Race*, saying, *Nichole, you are the last one to arrive. I'm sorry to tell you that you have been eliminated and you are not the winner of the Amazing Race.*

What if we were so close to that big defining moment and we don't reach it for one wrong move? What if we don't reach for it because of fear? What if we don't reach for it because we don't think we have what it takes?

If you think about it, aren't we all competing in one big "amazing race?" We truly are working together for one big purpose and one big prize, our very own Promised Land.

Paula Rinehart, author of *Strong Women Soft Hearts*, said, "It is easy to build small lives around the pain we encounter, to get lost in one thread of the plot of the story and miss the big theme." Too many of us get hung up in that one piece, or that one position and we lose sight of the big picture.

Mark Batterson followed up with the concept of one by saying, "You are only one defining decision away from a totally different life. One defining decision can change your trajectory and put you on a new path toward the Promised Land." We could let one position, one set of circumstances, derail us from fulfilling our purpose in life and from reaching our place of promise. Are you willing to take that chance?

*To walk out of God's will is to step into nowhere.* —C.S. Lewis

We all have a course set out for us, and for some of us it is going to be long and grueling. You can either take what has been given to you and finish your course strong . . .

Nichole Cornelius

and full of joy . . .

LiveStrong Half Marathon, Austin, TX, 2012

or you can quit the game altogether. The choice is ultimately up to you. If I could encourage you with anything, I would encourage you to stay in the game. The game is hard, the game is grueling, but the Promised Land is so worth it. Hang on. Keep moving. Never give up!

*For the more certain it is to you that God is painting on a big canvas and the picture is going to be beautiful beyond telling, the more willing you will be to hang in for the long haul.*—Paula Rinehart

# 4 THE OBJECT OF THE GAME

*Self-improvement is the name of the game, and your primary objective is to strengthen yourself, not to destroy an opponent.*—Maxwell Maltz

I am no expert on chess, but I have spent countless hours reading material on the game. I have gained an understanding of the complexity of the game, the meaning of the rules, the value of the pieces, and the ways in which those pieces move. I certainly do not expect you to become an expert on the game, as I would fail at that endeavor.

I hope by providing a basic foundation of chess, you will see the parallel between my life's experiences and your experiences, and how they both relate to the game. You will also see how each position is dependent on the one before and necessary for the purpose in our lives.

I first began my research by reading Patrick Wolff's *The Complete Idiot's Guide to Chess*. Since my knowledge was limited, this book seemed like the logical choice to bring me up to speed. Patrick Wolff describes chess as a game of war, strategy, and conquest. There are opponents to outlast and destroy. The winner and loser of the game are determined by skill, not luck. You have to train hard and play hard in order to win.

Chess is a fair game. There is no dice to roll and no umpires to regulate the game. All that is required is a desire to learn the rules and a willingness to play. You have to make decisions, decisions that are risky and costly. You cannot take a passive or back-seat approach if you plan on winning the game. You have to take chances and risks. You get involved, anticipate the moves of your opponent, and make decisions on moves even if they are wrong.

The game is based on skills and logic. Each piece has a set value and specific assigned movement (we will discuss this in a later chapter). This is critical for understanding the object of the game. The object is simple: render the opposing king powerless, otherwise known as checkmate, all the while protecting your own king. Checkmate occurs when the king is in a position to be captured (in check) or backed into a corner and cannot make any possible moves.

Chess carries the stigmatism that it is just for intellectuals and not very fun. It is true, the game is intimidating as there are so many rules of movement to learn, but I can assure you that there is a level of satisfaction every time you play. There is no greater feeling than capturing your opponent's pieces, getting promoted, and in the end, defeating your opponent once and for all.

There are three phases of chess: the opening phase, the middle phase, and the end phase. The opening phase of chess is over when the goal of the opening has been achieved: getting most of your pieces off their starting squares and the king into safety.

After successful completion of the goal, the game then moves to the middle phase, and the battle truly begins. During this phase, you should concentrate on attacking your opponent or fighting the attack of your opponent until you reach the end phase. The end phase is the final phase of the game. The transition to this phase may not be clear, but a visible sign is typically fewer pieces of higher value on the board.

If the objective in chess is to checkmate your opponent, what is the objective in life? While reading *A Million Miles in a Thousand Years* by Donald Miller, I came across this passage which made the connection to chess that much more real.

His friend Marco said, "Essentially, humans are alive for the purpose of a journey, a kind of three-act structure. They are born and spend several years discovering themselves in a world, then plod through a long middle in which they are compelled to search for a mate and reproduce and also create stability out of natural instability. Then, they find themselves at an ending that seems to be designed for reflection."

I love Marco's take on life. We are born, then we trod through life searching for our identity and love, and in the end, we reflect on all that we have done. That is how God created us to be. We have all been assigned tasks to carry out during our time on Earth. Some of us teach, some of us preach, some of us coach, heal, and entertain, and in the end, we reflect on the nature and the very being of God.

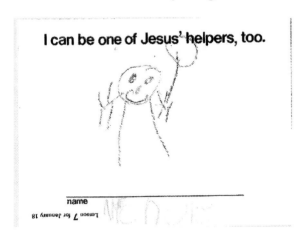

Highland Presbyterian Church Sunday school lesson, age 5

During a conversation captured in Exodus 33:18–22, Moses asked God to show His face. Moses wanted to *see*

Him. He wanted to make a personal connection to the God he served, loved, and obeyed. God responded by saying, "I will make all my goodness pass before you, and I will call out my name, Yahweh, before you. For I will show mercy to anyone I choose, and I will show compassion to anyone I choose, but you may not look directly at my face, for no one may see me and live."

How disheartening to not be able to put a face to someone you have a relationship with. All Moses wanted to do was to see God's face. I can understand Moses' desire to see God. I am a proof kind of girl, and I have struggled at times with not being able to see or touch God. The walking-by-faith approach is not always easy.

Maybe Moses, like me, needed tangible proof that God existed. I am not sure the exact reasons God would not reveal himself, but I have two reasons of my own. First of all, maybe God knows that if we can see Him, we will also try to control Him and manipulate Him. Secondly, maybe God would not let man see Him because everything man touches he has the ability to tarnish or destroy.

God is pure, God is holy, and God is perfect. The only way man can see God is to be pure at heart and no one is perfect. The only thing I know to be true is that having a relationship with God comes down to faith and faith comes by believing and *not* by seeing.

Since no one can see God's face or His glory directly, then how do we effectively do everything to the glory of God? What does glory look like? Christians utter words like "grace," "mercy," and "glory" so casually, but do we really understand what we mean? Do we have a real revelation of the word glory? If we did, wouldn't our lives reflect something totally different?

*Whether you eat or drink, or whatever you do, do all to the glory of God.*
—1 Corinthians 10:31

The article "Names of God" describes glory as an opinion,

estimation, or reputation in which one is held. God said that everything we do, down to what we eat and drink, is all for His glory. We reflect His presence, His name, and what principles He stands for so He can be seen by everyone *we* come in contact with.

We give God glory through praise, thanksgiving, obedience, respect, and service. We reflect God's glory by the way we respond to life: how we treat people, how we love them, and how we handle ourselves in midst of difficulties. Paul Tripp, author and speaker, said it best when he said, "I think my job is to make the grace of an invisible God, visible, wherever I am."

In all the years I have been walking with God, I firmly believe if He did not have a purpose for hardship, He would not allow it to happen. David Seamands, author of *Healing for Damaged Emotions,* confirmed my beliefs by saying that God will not allow anything to happen to us which by itself can defeat His ultimate purpose or defeat His children.

So, even though we go through hardships, those hardships will not ultimately defeat us. Too many of us lose sight that we will not be defeated. I know I am guilty of feeling that way. During painful times, it is hard to remember that those circumstances will not defeat us and the pain is only temporary.

Mark Batterson said, "We pray as if God's chief objective is our personal comfort. It's not. God's chief objective is His glory. And sometimes His gain involves a little pain." In order to avoid any kind of pain, we often pursue our own path. We get sidetracked from our purpose by pursuing our own happiness and desires without giving one thought to what the Lord has planned or what He desires. That simply goes against our created design.

I have to admit, I have pursued my own path for many, many years. When I finally gave into God's plan, I experienced blessings I never imagined. His plans have superseded my own. I assure you, what is waiting for you in the Promised Land, whether it is joy, peace, or love, will amaze you. However, you cannot achieve all this without experiencing some form of pain.

Harbour Town Lighthouse, in Hilton Head, South Carolina, is one of the most popular landmarks on the island. It has been described as the centerpiece of the Sea Pines Plantation. The tower is 90 feet tall and has various stops along the way to the top that display historic events that have occurred in Hilton Head. At the top of the lighthouse lies a tiny shop. The area around the lighthouse is very charming, filled with live music and little outdoor eateries and quaint shops.

Harbour Town Lighthouse, Memorial Day weekend 2012

I love lighthouses and what they symbolize: a light to guide us along the way. We are like lighthouses casting a light to lost and troubled souls to guide them safely to God. Every experience, every heartbreak, every disappointment, and every decision to move forward regardless of the situation is an opportunity for God's glory, or His light, to be seen by the world.

We are the light of the world whether we want the spotlight or not. People are watching our every move in what we say and how we respond to what life throws our way. We are a billboard for God as Joyce Meyer says. If I were driving down the highway and ran across your billboard, what would it say? What would you be advertising? Are you advertising defeat and sorrow or happiness and joy? Is your billboard appealing or distracting?

People are desperate for inspiration and happiness as the world is full of despair. I hope your message is inspiring, motivating, and full of hope. I hope you have something positive to give back to the world and you give reasons to never give up and to be an overcomer. Like Nelson Mandela said, "I hope you let your own light shine so you unconsciously give other people permission to do the same."

*Maybe the journey isn't so much about becoming anything. Maybe it's about un-becoming everything that isn't really you so you can be who you were meant to be in the first place.*—Unknown

# 5 THE PLAYERS OF THE GAME

*After the game, the king and the pawn go into the same box.*—Italian Proverb

**The Chess Set**

Chess comes with a standard set of pieces known as the chess set. The chess set consists of one king, one queen, two rooks, two bishops, two knights, and eight pawns in colors such as black, white, and even red like in my own personal chess board.

Pictured from left to right: pawn, rook, knight, bishop, queen, and king

The pawn is worth one point in value. To put it into simpler terms, pawns are given a value of one and all other pieces are valued in terms of how many pawns they are worth. For example, bishops and knights are worth three pawns, rooks are worth five pawns, and queens are worth nine pawns. The king, however, can never be exchanged, so losing your king essentially means the game is over.

Patrick Wolff, author of *The Complete Idiot's Guide to Chess*, describes the pawn as the foot soldier of your army of pieces. This piece typically engages the enemy face to face and receives the brunt of the war. The pawn is so low on the scale it is not even considered a piece that is why it is called the pawn.

The pawn may be considered the least valued and least powerful piece, but it is still important. There are eight pawns in the game with eight times the opportunity to advance in the game. This actually sets you up with an advantage if you play your pieces right.

The rook was originally created to symbolize a warrior's chariot, but later evolved to look like a castle's tower. He stands beside the king and queen and serves to protect them. He is strong like the castle's wall that he imitates.

The knight resembles a horse's head and moves by jumping over the other pieces. A disadvantage for the knight is that it is a long-range piece. Even though it moves through each position quickly, it takes longer for it to get to where it needs to be.

The bishop represents the church and resembles a bishop's head garment. In Medieval Europe, the bishop was second in line next to the king and queen. The bishop follows the same rank in chess. The bishop moves quickly across the board, but can easily be blocked.

The queen is the advisor of the king, and she stands beside him in life and in the game. She is the most powerful piece because she has no conditions on how she can move. Lastly, the king is the male monarch whose capture is the object of the game. He is a wise ruler, but not a warrior. He is often stationary, but well surrounded.

The chess pieces are similar to people we surround ourselves with: friends, acquaintances, family, church family, and co-workers. We have allies, a support system, and we have enemies, those who bring us down and ultimately want to destroy us. It's sad, but it's true. We should give careful consideration to those we surround ourselves with. Can they be trusted? What are their intentions? Are they supportive, or are they there to cause us harm?

Sometimes your chess set might come with some surprises: people you never expected to collide with and people you spent your whole life running from. Like God parted the Red Sea for Moses, He can split your board wide open and plop someone down with no regards to how you feel. He can line you up with the unexpected. He can line you up with people who are invasive and persistent. He can align you with loud people and those that are direct. He can and He will align you with agents of change.

For many years, I kept a great deal of space on my board open to toxic relationships. I was a people pleaser and did not have the heart to cut them out as I felt it was not the "Christian" thing to do. I believed in them and their ability to change, so I had a very hard time letting them go. My wise friend Sherry once told me that I can have people like this in my life, but they don't need much space. I can keep them around, but at a distance. Maybe you should consider the same.

*As with any journey, who you travel with can be more important than your destination.* —Lovendar.com

## The Enemy of the Game

*Know your enemy and learn about his favorite sport.*—Nelson Mandela

There are times in my life when it is hard for me to figure out who the real enemy is. Is it me? Is it God? Is it the Devil himself? These are questions that I wrestle with constantly. In the book, *A Million Miles in a Thousand Years,* Donald Miller describes Satan as a force in the world that doesn't want us to live the good stories. It doesn't want us to face our issues, to face our fear, and bring something beautiful into the world. So, he fights us on a daily basis and no tactic is beneath him. His main purpose is to bring opposition to the plan of God: kill, steal, and destroy.

The enemy is constantly changing like the positions in the game. He calculates every move he makes because he wants you out of your position and ultimately out of the game. He believes that we can be easily manipulated into executing his plan, and he will stop at nothing to do so. He will use any device, plan, procedure, or technique to accomplish his mission.

He plants seeds of doubt. He uses pawns to do his dirty work: inflicting pain on others. He deploys friends, family, co-workers, and sometimes the ones we feel closest to and trust the most. His plan is to use these people to distract us from our purpose in life. If we are not careful, his plan will shift the course we find ourselves on and it could also cost us our destiny.

In chess, our piece becomes the opponent when it is sitting in a position that another one of our pieces would like to move to. Sometimes the best way to get the blocking piece out of the way is to sacrifice it. This is called clearance sacrifice.

You might think the enemy is attacking you, when, in fact, you are the enemy. We are quick to blame the attack on someone else, when actually, we need to simply conquer ourselves. Maybe you struggle with lying, jealousy, anger, bitterness, or fear.

Sometimes the best move we can make is to sacrifice ourselves. God may have to execute a "clearance sacrifice" to rid ourselves of pride, ego, or actions that give the opponent another advantage.

Often times, we blame God and end up resenting Him when things don't go our way or our prayers go unanswered. We didn't get the job or the promotion. The contract on the house fell through. The diagnosis came back positive. We lost custody of our kids. Our spouse walked out the door.

Mark Batterson said, "If God answered our selfish prayers, they would actually short-circuit the purposes of God in our lives. We would fail to learn the lessons God is trying to teach us or cultivate the character God is trying to shape in us." So in turn, our unanswered prayers turn God into the enemy when He has nothing but the absolute best planned out for us.

*Like a good chess player, Satan is always trying to maneuver you into a position where you can save your castle only by losing your bishop.*— C.S. Lewis

## The Main Player of the Game

*Since it is so likely that children will meet cruel enemies, let them at least have heard of brave knights and heroic courage.*—C.S. Lewis

I talked about what makes up your chess set and the enemy, but we cannot forget about the main player of the game. Every great story has a main character, someone who wants something and overcomes conflict to get it, as Donald Miller describes in the book, *A Million Miles in a Thousand Years*. A character has to face his greatest fears along the way. In the game of life, we are the main character of the story. Whether we are the pawn, the knight, the rook, the bishop, the queen, or the king, we all play a part.

In this game, I can identify with all the pieces, but primarily I identify with the pawn. From my early childhood, I battled with insecurities as well as low self-esteem and worthlessness. After years of hearing insults and harsh words like, you are stupid, fat, and ugly, I finally started believing them and those words became my identity.

Those insecurities traveled with me most of my life. They affected the way I carried myself, and how I interacted with other people. I ran away from the spotlight and tried my best to remain hidden. Very seldom did I want to be chosen for anything. I guess I settled for supporting roles instead of any leading roles.

*Sometimes the hardest part of the journey is believing you are worthy of the trip.*—Glenn Beck

When I think about being chosen, my mind drifts back to the playground of my elementary school, Holiday Park, and the dreadful game of Red Rover. *Red rover red rover, send Nichole right over* echo in my mind as if it were yesterday. The anguish of the decision—will they pick me or not—tormented my mind. When I was chosen, it was only because I was the weakest link or so I thought. So I settled into defeat, ran half-heartedly, and failed to break the chain-linked arms.

Even though on the outside it appeared that I did not want to be chosen, I secretly did on the inside. When I was not chosen, my feelings got hurt because I felt rejected. In the devotion, "Getting Picked," Os Hillman explains,

*Most of us growing up either landed on the "picked" or the "unpicked" side of life. It is awesome to be picked by the God of the universe to be on His team. When God chose you, He knew what He was doing. God doesn't always pick those who have the greatest skill, the greatest aptitude, or even the greatest personality. However, He always has something in mind for those He picks.*

Moses was chosen to lead the Israelites out of 400 years of slavery and lead them to the Promised Land. David, a young shepherd boy, was chosen to defeat the giant Goliath. Ester was chosen to save her people from execution. The Virgin Mary was chosen as the Mother of Jesus Christ.

We are all chosen by God to do something great for Him, and we all have a part to play. He chooses us to carry out the big stuff in life and sometimes the "big" stuff is the hard stuff, the stuff nobody wants to deal with: sickness, betrayal, loss, and abuse.

*As Jesus was walking along, he saw a man who had been blind from birth. 'Rabbi,' his disciples asked him, 'why was this man born blind? Was it because of his own sins or his parents' sins?'*

*'It was not because of his sins or his parents' sins,' Jesus answered. 'This happened so the power of God could be seen in him. We must quickly carry out the tasks assigned us by the one who sent us. The night is coming, and then no one can work. But while I am here in the world, I am the light of the world.'*—John 9:1–5 (NLT)

The world is looking for authentic and brave people who make it in life, who can overcome obstacles and who vow to never give up. The beauty of God is that He chooses us not based on our ability, but because of our weakness. We may never break through the chains in Red Rover on our own, but together with God's power we can.

*The world needs for us to have courage.*—Robert McKee

My paternal grandmother, Marie, was the leading character in my life. Not only did she make the most amazing buttermilk pancakes, she was a seamstress and her specialty was patchwork quilts. She took scraps of fabric and patched them together to create her quilts. The scraps were worn, the edges were frayed, and the color patterns were hard on the eyes, but somehow she formed something beautiful. To this day, one of her quilts remains on my bed. It provides me warmth, comfort, and is a token of the life I had with her.

My grandmother was more than a seamstress; she was my rock and my role model. If I could spend every waking moment with her, I would. I loved to be with her. My dad lived with my grandma for several years. On my weekends to stay with my dad, he was often found outside helping my uncle repair cars.

I spent the majority of my time with my grandmother. We could be found sitting outside on her bright orange swing, or we could be found inside playing card games. We played War, Rummy, and Blackjack. I think she is the main reason I love to play games.

I was the only granddaughter in the family, and I honestly believe I was the apple of her eye. She paid special attention to me and kept a close eye on me. She could smell foul play the moment I ran into the house screaming and crying. Troy and David were notorious for dangling my Cabbage Patch kid on the clothesline. Years later when Grandma got a dryer, my Cabbage Patch kid would be often found in the dryer getting her "wrinkles" out. It's a wonder my doll survived; I guess she was resilient like me.

Grandma was the essence of strength, a woman of dignity and integrity, who knew that laughter was the medicine for the soul. She endured so much from burying a young husband, raising four hellish boys on her own, and surviving breast cancer, until her heart gave out in the end. No one could fully replace the void she left after she was gone.

In looking back, I know why God chose her to be my grandmother. I needed to witness, first hand, a woman of courage and strength, who could love without fail. I needed a protector and a *pattern* in which to follow. She did all that for me and more. She set the stage for me. She was honest and hardworking: a fighter and a survivor, never the victim.

I am sure life was extremely hard for her, but never did she show it. All I remember is the sacrifice she made for me and just about anyone she came in contact with. She made people feel special, and she made them smile. She was flawless like the quilts she made.

That is how I see the experiences and the people that make up our lives. There are some that take away from our lives, and there are some that add something positive to it. Some people are harsh, mean, and direct. Some people are spiteful and abusive. Others are uplifting, encouraging, and respectful. Each person we encounter is like a scrap of fabric, sewn together, to create the blanket of our life. We need them all, the good and the bad. It's how we shape our character. It's how we reach our destiny.

*You couldn't become the servant God is calling you to be without the threads of your past being knitted into the Technicolor fabric of your future.*—Beth Moore, *The Beloved Disciple*

So, I'll ask you to consider the following questions: What does your chess set look like? Who are you associating with? Are they supporting you and building you up, or are they tearing you down and leading you towards defeat? Are you willing to move some people around so you can position yourself with success and people who are positive?

Maybe you need to take inventory of the space on your board and make some adjustments. It might be time to close some doors and leave people behind. You need to line yourself up with people who will support you and pick you up when you fall. You need people who will believe in you and encourage you in your time of need. You absolutely need this line of defense if you are going to win your game.

Not only do you need a good defense, but you should accept the part that you have been given. Be the main character of your story. Be the one who wants something and overcomes conflict to get it. Be someone's hero. Be someone's inspiration. Live a better story.

*Small streams don't plan to become mighty rivers. We just move in a direction; God decides what He'll have us become.* —Bob Goff

# 6 THE RULES OF MOVEMENT

*If you're going to play the game properly, you'd better know every rule.—*
Barbara Jordan

## Rules of Movement

With any game comes rules, and chess is no different. Rules instruct us on how to play the game. Rules provide direction and bring order and fairness. Without them, there would be no point in playing. Rules are hard to learn, and some people don't like to follow them. I am a rule follower by nature and very seldom do I break any rules. The fear of consequences for breaking rules was instilled in me at a very early age.

However, if I find myself in a situation where I feel as if I am being controlled or manipulated by someone and their rules, I am not so eager to follow them. Panic starts to set in, and I have been known to kick and scream and throw my childlike tantrums before I gave in, if I even gave in at all.

According to chess.com, the white piece always moves first. Alternately, the players take turns moving one piece at a time. A player has to move every time, skipping a turn is not an option. Each piece has its own rules for moving. The pawn has two basic moves: move without capture and move with capture. Moving without capture is simply moving to another square (advancing in the game), but not capturing another piece. Moving with capture is capturing another piece. Here is how the pieces move.

- The pawn captures one square diagonally in front to the left or right.
- The pawn moves one square straight ahead except for the very first move. At this time, the pawn can move forward two squares.
- The knight is the only piece that does not move in a straight line. It moves in an "L" shape.
- The knight can also jump over the other pieces just as the horse it resembles.
- The bishop moves diagonally and it only moves on the squares of the same color as it starts on.
- The rook can move forwards, backwards, and to the sides, but cannot move diagonally.
- The queen can move in any one straight direction: forwards, backwards, sideways, or diagonally, and as far as possible as long as it does not move through any of its own pieces.
- The king can only move one square in any direction: forwards, backwards, to the sides, and diagonally.
- The king has one special move that is called castling. On its very first move, the king can move either two squares to the right or two squares to the left. Castling moves the king into a safer position.

Chess pieces move according to rules and logic, but we tend to move based on thoughts and emotions. We make moves based out of fear, guilt, shame, and anger. These thoughts and emotions can paralyze us and halt our movement altogether. The hardest concept to grasp is to trust the position God has placed you in whether it is unemployment, sickness, or loss, or any other hard position you find yourself in.

When we don't like our present circumstances, we often cry out: *I don't like living here. I can't stand this job. Why isn't anything working out for me?* Maybe God has you right where you are so He can work something out of you. Maybe God has placed you where you are so you can help someone else through a difficult situation of their own. There are reasons for the positions you find yourself in.

Hafiz said, "The place where you are right now, God circled on a map for you." If you are not moving, then there is a reason for you staying. God is big enough to move you if He wants to. The path He leads you down may include the long way around and it may be filled with many starts and stops. Remember, God will never "short-circuit" the trip if there is something for you to learn or work out.

What I want you to take away from learning about the movement of the pieces is how it relates to life. God never wants us to move backwards. He is always trying to get us to forget the past and move forward (Philippians 3:12-14 NLT). There will be times when we have to take leaps of faith. Our movement may not always be linear, or in a straight line. However, in order to follow God's plan for our lives, we have to be flexible and we have to be willing to move.

*In God's direction of travel, He only gives you one—forward.— Unknown*

Moses was chosen specifically by God to lead the Israelites out of Egypt and into the Promised Land. The Israelites were beginning to grow rapidly in number which frightened Pharaoh, the King of Egypt. He enslaved them for roughly 400 years.

The map below shows the exodus or the departure of the Israelites from Egypt to the Promised Land. The Land of Goshen is where the Israelites lived and was considered to be the best in Egypt as it was suitable for growing crops and livestock. However, the Israelites population grew in number and the Egyptians feared that they would be overpowered. Out of this fear, the Egyptians enslaved the Israelites and forced them to build treasured cities.

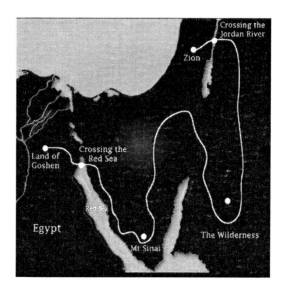

The intended route to the Promised Land should have only taken 11 days; however, the journey took 40 years. God knew how the Israelites would react to the journey so He led them through the wilderness. Moses and the Israelites left the land of Goshen stopping at 41 places until they reached their last stop in Moab.

From Moab, the Israelites were ready to cross into the land of Canaan, the Promised Land, but first they had to cross the Jordan River. Moses led the Israelites up until his death. After he died, Joshua was appointed to lead the Israelites across the Jordan River.

*You'll never get a promise without positioning. The wilderness is positioning for the Promised Land.*—Denny Livingston

## The Crossing

The Jordan River forms the boundary between the country of Jordan and the West Bank. It was the place that stood between the Israelites and the Promised Land. In order to step foot into the land, they had to cross the Jordan River and destroy the inhabitants of the land. However, the Israelites refused to enter the land because they were terrified of their enemies.

When Joshua came face to face with the Jordan River, I imagine he had great fear. Could he handle the mighty Jordan River and lead his people across? The task must have been daunting. Just how strong was the current? What lay beneath that calm and peaceful surface? What if in fear, he turned back and missed out on the Promised Land?

I know I am guilty of reacting out of fear, and I bet there are many of you reading this that do the same. We don't have the courage to take the first terrifying step into the unknown, so out of fear, we turn back to the "wilderness" just like the Israelites did.

*You have to walk a great distance to achieve something of value.*— Steven Spielberg

The Little River runs alongside the library in my hometown and throughout the city. There is a path of stepping stones to use to cross over to the other side of the river at this particular spot. As a child, the highlight of my trip to the library was playing on those stones. Those stones provided excitement and a way for me to *leap* through life and *skip* ahead.

Little River Park

The movement of chess is similar. There are times when we can skip over other pieces and positions, and there are times we have to take each step that is given. The stones we must cross vary from person to person. For me, I had to cross through positions of risk, defeat, and despair to reach the permanent position of freedom, stability, and love.

Your stones may not look like mine, but I know you have had to cross some stones and will have many more to cross in the future. In *Beauty for Ashes*, Joyce Meyer said, "The only way out is through." She described the doorway of freedom as this,

> *I now understand that in order to be led out of bondage and into freedom, we must pass back through the same, or similar, doorways of pain that we previously went through so that we can get on the other side of them. When we are taken into bondage through doorways of pain, we must pass through the same*

*doorways to get out of its captivity. Both times through the doorways are painful, first from the actual abuse, and again from the memory of it. In order to deliver and to heal us, the Lord must lead us to face issues, people, and the truths that we find difficult, if not impossible, to face on our own.*

We are like the Israelites in the fact that we have to cross through our "Jordan" to the land of freedom and victory. We have to cross through positions of conflict, deceit, loss, and betrayal in order to be delivered. Like the Israelites, some people don't have the courage to go through to the other side and find themselves stationary and unable to move through their pain.

There is great fear in digging up the past and digging into the truth. It is much easier to stay in our place of comfort and security. The process of walking through requires us to come to terms with the truth of who we are and why we act the way we do. It forces us to turn the mirror towards our inner "demons" and understand why we sometimes act the way we do.

I have faced many hard truths about myself. The truth was very painful to swallow. As I began to trust God through the process of uncovering the truth, I realized that the "other side," the healing, was all worth any pain I had to endure.

*Most obstacles melt away when we make up our minds to walk boldly through them.*—Orison Swett Marden

In December 2011, my friends, Rachele, Sherry, and I went hiking along the Ramsey Cascades in Gatlinburg, Tennessee. The hike was a total of four hours. It took two hours to get to the waterfall and two hours back. A four-hour hike was very challenging for me as I was not in the greatest of shape. Our reward at the end of the hike would be a 90-foot waterfall.

The trail was rugged and covered with exposed tree roots. There was no tour guide and no directional signs to follow.

The worn-down path was the only guide we had to follow. Being the novice hiker, I failed to pack water and snacks. I really had no true concept of what the adventure entailed. As expected, I began to tire out. I wanted to give up actually. My feet were hurting and my knees were aching. I was out of shape and not cut out for this hike.

As we approached the waterfall, I stopped and decided the trip was not worth it. My friends did their best to encourage me to keep going, but their attempts failed. They went on, and I sat there feeling defeated. A few minutes into my pity party, an elderly, frail man passed me by. As he walked past me, he said, "The view is stunning, and it's totally worth it." He was not in the best of shape either. I could tell by the use of his walking stick.

In that moment, I thought, why can't I do this? He was not letting his physical limitations stop him so why am I letting my emotional limitations stop me? The journey came with a few more challenges as I was greeted with this sign.

*Warning, 4 deaths have happened here. Death? Don't be next?* I didn't sign up for the threat of death. I was expecting a leisurely stroll to be one with nature and catch a glimpse of a waterfall at the end-of the-rainbow kind of adventure, and not some tight-rope walking, boulder-scaling, near-death experience.

If you think about it, this is like the path of life. There are hills to climb and rocks to scale over, but somewhere between the obstacles of life, lies a sense of adventure, excitement, and a little risk to reach a stunning reward at the end.

Photo credit: http://www.hikinginthesmokys.com/ramsay.htm

While the picture fails to capture the waterfall's beauty, it is still breathtaking. Could you imagine the regret I would have had if I had not gone through to the other side? What if I had let fear have the final say in this journey?

I bet if we could get a glimpse of what the "other side" looked like, then we would all take the journey. We would fight through the pain, the heartache, the fear, and the affliction, because of what is waiting for us on the other side.

Let me ask you this. What does your Jordan look like? You may not be leading a nation of people through a river into the Promised Land, but you have something to cross through. Maybe your "Jordan" is simply getting out of the bed and showing up in life.

Maybe your "Jordan" is facing your past and overcoming the demons that haunt you on a daily basis. Maybe your "Jordan" is moving across the country so you can fight to be with your kids. Maybe your "Jordan" is picking up the pieces after you failed miserably and it cost you your career. Maybe your "Jordan" is simply to forgive yourself of past mistakes and to let go. Maybe your "Jordan" is to embrace your uniqueness, whether it be perceived as weirdness by others, and be the person you were created to be.

*Some people spend their entire lives on the eastern shore of the Jordan waiting for God to part the river, while God waits for them to get their feet wet.*—Mark Batterson

You may cross the Jordan once in your lifetime or many, many times. There are some days I feel like I live in the Jordan. I have even considered grabbing a raft and floating around because the shore is nowhere to be found. Will I ever get across? How many more times do I have to cross before I am finally on the other side?

Just when I think I am done, another "Jordan" is awaiting me. I am exhausted, worn out, and defeated; I want to quit altogether. However, I keep walking. I keep crossing. I keep fighting through my circumstances and put one foot in front of the other in search of the Promised Land. I keep moving because I believe in something greater ahead.

If I were to draw a map of my own journey, I am sure the image would be similar to the map of the Israelites: long and drawn out. There would be instances where I circled around the same mountains over and over again because of failing the test the first time.

I am quite confident that there was a quicker and easier route that I could have taken, and I know my own resistance, my fear, and my lack of trust are partially to blame. However, God knew what was inside of me, and He led me down this long and drawn-out path for a reason.

Just as a child will never know the concept of hot until he or she touches a hot stove, we will not truly get revelation until we physically go through the process. In order for us to receive revelation, sometimes God has to move us into positions that get our attention. In the devotion "How God Makes Fishermen," Os Hillman explains,

*Sooner or later, God calls you into relationship with Him. For many, like Paul, it comes through dramatic encounters like being knocked off a horse, blinded and spoken to personally by God. Some people are more difficult than others to reach and so require this level of crisis. This is a time when God requires major changes so that you follow Him fully. It can be a time in which God harnesses years of experience for a new life purpose.*

As you continue on with me, you will see that I found myself in a level of crisis just like Paul experienced. I was not blinded per se, but God spoke directly to me through several painful circumstances. He left me no other choice but to follow Him. It was through these painful times, I was able to finally cross over into my place of promise.

If you find yourself standing at the edge of your Jordan, take a step, and place your foot in the water. You have a 90-foot breathtaking waterfall waiting for you. Don't stop here. The journey is far from over. You have a place of promise to reach. It is simply waiting for you to cross over.

*It's your road, and yours alone. Others may walk it with you, but no one can walk it for you.*—Rumi

# 7 THE STRATEGIES
# OF THE GAME

*In every aspect of life, have a game plan, and then do your best to achieve it.*—Alan Kulwicki

We covered the design and the object of the game and the players involved, and now we need to learn how to actually play the game. There are specific patterns a player must follow for playing the game. If you are going to win, you need to have a clear expectation of what you want and a strong desire to complete it. Zig Ziglar said, "If you don't see yourself as a winner, you cannot perform as a winner."

There are no random moves in chess. You must have a strategy and a plan for how you will play the game. You have to set up your opening moves so you don't leave any important pieces vulnerable. You set the pieces up to attack your opponent all at the same time. Your moves must be thought out and calculated. You have to consider how every move is going to affect the others. What will happen if I make that move? What will happen if I don't?

The article "Checkmate Patterns in Chess" states that very few games end with checkmate or the impending threat of a checkmate, so the game must come to a draw. In order for the player to get practice with checkmate, he or she should practice with checkmate patterns. If a winner cannot be declared, what is the purpose of playing? The purpose of playing is to get stronger in strategic plays.

The article "Checkmate Patterns in Chess" also identified 10 basic checkmate patterns that every player should know or at least make an attempt to know. I will only cover a couple. The back-rank mate occurs when a rook or queen checkmates a king that is blocked mainly by pawns. The smothered mate happens when a king is too well defended for his own good. The king is sitting in the corner of the board and covered by his own pieces, but is attacked by a knight that can jump over the other pieces. The king has no other moves to make and checkmate occurs.

This move may seem impossible, but a lowly pawn can checkmate a king (a king and a pawn checkmate). A pawn that is close to promoting (discussed in a later chapter) can divert the king from protecting himself. The king is so focused on trying to stop the pawn from promoting that he gets trapped himself. I find this opportunity exciting. A lowly pawn can move up the ranks of life and capture a king. It makes me feel that anything is possible. Don't you?

Not only do you need to familiarize yourself with checkmate patterns, but you need to learn strategic moves as well. Chess is a game of skill, not luck. If you are going to improve your game, you need to practice and know which strategies are effective.

The author of *50 Strategies to Gain the Upper Hand Over Your Opponent* states that you first need to know your plan of action. What do you plan to accomplish based on the strengths and weaknesses of your and your opponent's position? What is your goal?

- Throughout the game, you should lead your pieces more effectively than your opponent.
- Evaluate your moves in order to prevent a potential threat from the opponent.
- Try to avoid splitting pawns into isolated groups. They are stronger in a chain.
- Think before moving pawns forward because they cannot move backwards. The enemy may try to lure you to advance your pawns to create weaknesses in your pieces.
- The queen is the most powerful piece, but needs a rook and other minor pieces to be effectively used.
- Try to castle the king as early as possible.

There are lots of strategies to consider, but they will develop with time and practice. Focus on your goal, checkmating your opponent's king, and how you will achieve that goal. What moves are you planning to make to ensure that you have met your goal? You must be quick, strong, and reactive to what your opponent brings. You've got to "fake out" your opponent, scare him, make him hesitate, and second guess his moves. This applies to both defense and offense.

The best move to make is to improve your position on the board and attack your opponent's position in ways that do not involve checkmate. In order to do this, you need to understand tactics or sequences of moves that limit your opponent's options in the game.

- Don't launch a premature attack. Develop your pieces so they will support each other.
- Drive the enemy king to the edge or corner of the board.
- Be ahead of your opponent. Capture more of your opponent's pieces before he captures yours.

- If you end up cornered in the end game, look for ways to get into a position of stalemate or draw.
- Have the material advantage or have more pieces to attack with.
- You should develop the ability to "see" any position which pieces and pawns are attacking and which ones are being attacked.
- You should always evaluate and calculate the risk of a capture and assess whether the result will give you the material advantage or not.
- You can strengthen these skills by studying different positions of attack.
- Move, defend, or block the piece that is being attacked.
- Capture the piece that is attacking your piece or attack another one.

*You have to learn the rules of the game and then you have to play better than anyone else.*—Albert Einstein

In September 2008, Suzanne Collins released the book, *The Hunger Games*. This was the first book of the *Hunger Games* trilogy. The *Hunger Games* is a young adult science fiction novel based on a 16-year-old girl named Katniss who is willing to sacrifice her life on behalf of her younger sister to play in the Hunger Games.

This is an annual televised game of survival in which 13 girls and 13 boys between the ages of 12 to 18 fight each other until there is only one survivor. The winner receives the food and other necessities for their district for a year.

The plot of this book is unsettling and disturbing: children forced to fight each other, yet, I was intrigued. By staying with the story, I found a spirit of determination in this young character. It shows the true nature of a fighter, a warrior, and an overcomer. Katniss' only weapon was her bow and arrow, and she could not use the arrows foolishly.

She also had to be quick on her feet, aware of her surroundings, and not succumb to a moment of weakness. She knew the benefits of rationing her food versus consuming it all at once. She knew who to trust and who not to. She also knew the importance of taking the time to stop and rest. She had her eye on the prize and that prize was surviving. She would not let any opponent get in her way.

Katniss was smart and cunning, and she learned survival skills while spending time hunting with her father. We must have the same spirit that Katniss has if we are going to live in the world we live in today. We have an adversary whose prime mission is to kill, steal, and destroy. He does not want us happy or successful. He does not want us making a difference.

He wants to stop us dead in our tracks, terrorize our mind with depression, and leave us with no hope. He wants nothing more than to destroy us. I know this because he has fought me every step of the way, and I positioned myself to be a warrior like Katniss. I knew the importance of spending time with God, learning His ways, His word, and how He handles his opponents.

There is no aspect of the world that is certain or secure. The job market is not secure. One day you are working, and the next you are standing in the unemployment line. One day you are paying your mortgage, and the next day your house is in foreclosure. One day you are healthy, and the next day you are left with a debilitating illness. In every aspect of our life, we are being attacked and there are some battles we cannot fight on our own. It's like swimming in shark-infested waters.

Not only do we need physical weapons, we need spiritual ones too. The Apostle Paul said, "Be strong in the Lord and in the power of His might. Put on the whole armor of God, that you may be able to stand against the wiles of the Devil (Ephesians 6:10-11)."

- Stand therefore, having girded your waist with truth.
- Put on the breastplate of righteousness.
- Shod your feet with the preparation of the gospel of peace.
- Take the shield of faith with which you will be able to quench all the fiery darts of the wicked one.
- Take the helmet of salvation, and the sword of the Spirit, which is the word of God.
- Always with all prayer and supplication in the Spirit.
- Be watchful to this end with all perseverance and supplication for all the saints.

*The opportunity to secure ourselves against defeat lies in our own hands, but the opportunity of defeating an enemy is provided in the enemy himself.*—Sun Tzu

When I was a young child, my dad lived in Nashville, Tennessee, and I would visit him some weekends. The trip to Tennessee always included a visit to Chuck E Cheese and a chance to play my beloved Whac-A-Mole. In case you are not aware, Whac-A-Mole is a game that has a cabinet with holes in the top. Each hole holds a little mole that randomly pops up and down. The object of the game is to hit the moles on the head with a mallet and force them back down in the hole.

In the game of life, we are constantly trying to dodge the moles that the enemy sends our way. The enemy knows what bothers you and what upsets you. Typically these moles "pop" up during times of stress, those weak moments in your life, so he can knock you off your game.

You may be asking yourself why you should learn all these rules and strategies for chess. How does this apply to your life? I am trying to get you to think like a warrior. You face battles every day. The more experience you have in dealing with conflict, confrontation, mishaps, and the unexpected, the more you are ready to deal with whatever is waiting for you around the corner and pops up along the way.

There are so many facets of playing the game of chess. You must be ready, and you must be prepared because the enemy is waiting to devour you. You may not be able to visibly see him, but he is there waiting to strike. By learning the tactics of your opponent and ways to strengthen your strategy, you set yourself up for success and if not success, movement ahead in life. The enemy fights us through our circumstances, but primarily he is after our mind. He knows that if he can get inside our head, then he can take our thoughts captive and use those thoughts to defeat us. That is why you constantly have to be on guard, quick on your feet, and aware of your surroundings. You have to stay ahead of him by standing on the truth of God's word, live in peace, pray, and persevere. As they say in the show *Survivor*, you have to outwit, outplay, and outlast. Now, let's play the game.

*I knew that if I allowed fear to overtake me, my journey was doomed. Fear, to a great extent, is born of a story we tell ourselves, and so I chose to tell myself a different story from the one women are told. I decided I was safe. I was strong. I was brave. Nothing could vanquish me.*— Cheryl Strayed, *Wild*

# PHASE ONE: THE CHESS OPENING:

## *LET THE GAMES BEGIN*

# 8 THE STARTING POSITION

*Each player must accept the cards life deals him or her. But once they are in hand, he or she alone must decide how to play the cards in order to win the game.*—Voltaire

The opening phase of chess consists of the first 8 to 12 moves of the game. At the start of the game, the pieces line up according to their starting position. Beginning from left to

right, each player's pieces line up in the order of rook, knight, bishop, queen, king, bishop, knight, and rook. The second row houses the eight pawns.

David A. Wheeler, author of *A Beginner's Garden of Chess Openings*, states that the first move is crucial for setting the tone of the game. He said that careful consideration should be taken when making the first move. The first moves of a chess game are coined the "opening" or "opening moves."

Starting with a good opening move will provide better protection of the king and will give you more control over the center of the board. This will also provide more mobility of the pieces and possible opportunities to capture opposing pawns and other pieces.

To be successful in this phase, you should focus on moving the center pawns first. You want to move the lesser-valued pieces before the higher-valued pieces and castle early, or safeguard the king. Castling quickly moves the king out of the center and into one of the corners. The king will be out of the way of the other pieces and allows the development of the rook.

If rooks are going to have an opportunity to play the game and attack other pieces, they are going to need open files, or paths in which to move. Rooks need these open files to position themselves to protect the king and queen. When pawns move forward or are exchanged, they create the needed open files.

Immediately, we see a power struggle over who is going to control the center of the board, the white or the black player. One popular first move is to have the white player move the king two spaces into the space designated as "E4." Immediately the player begins to start controlling the center of the board, and it also frees up the queen and the bishop.

The black player is then left with two options. He can mirror the white player's move by moving the king into space "E5," or he can make a move that leads to other openings, such as executing the Sicilian Defense, a move that causes immediate attack of the center.

The French Defense is a strategy where the black player allows the white player to have more control of the center of the board. The black player can choose the Pirc/Modern move, which allows the white player to take the center with the plan to ruin white's wonderful reputation.

The first moves in chess set the tone for the game and this can be expected in life. When I think of "opening moves," my mind wanders back to the game Trouble I used to play as a child. The object of the game was to have all four of your pieces move out of home and around the board to reach the finish line first. In order to move out of home, you had to click on the pop-o-matic dice and land on a six. Without fail, I could never land on a six and get out of home. I felt that way in life too.

*The story of your life is the story of the long and brutal assault on your heart by the one who knows what you can be and fears it.*—John Eldredge

My story began with trouble one sweltering hot July afternoon in 1975. My mom who was just seven-months pregnant with me had stopped over at my Granny's house to finish up some laundry. My cousins Troy and David were along for the ride and were off playing in the back of the house. When it was time to leave, my mom could not find the boys, who were hiding on purpose.

Instead of finding them, she stumbled across the lifeless body of her older sister, my aunt Trina, lying on the floor. In that moment, my aunt was gone. *What? Trina was gone? Who would have done this and why? She was too young to die. Who was going to care for my cousin Shelly who was only one and half years old at the time?* Trina who was only 19 was just a child herself.

The sudden death of Trina shook our family to the core, and that set the tone of my family's life from there on out. My Granny and my Papaw Jim grieved the loss of their daughter Trina, and their sudden reconnection enraged Granny's current husband, Johnny Wilson, known by us as

J.W.

He was a sick individual, and I am not talking in the physical sense. He was controlling and very angry at times. He took that rage out on Shelly and me in the form of sexual abuse. While I am not condoning his actions toward my cousin and me, I do know that hurting people hurt people whether intentional or not.

The abuse began when I was five and Shelly was seven. Here we are pictured around that age on a trip to the lake, and of course, I am in the driver's seat. A few years into the abuse, Shelly finally found the courage to come forth and tell on J.W. I remember the day all too well.

Shelly and I were sitting next to each other on Granny's plush brown couch. Granny sat next to Shelly, and J.W. sat in the rocking chair directly in front of us. I remember the tense pressure my hands felt from gripping the couch and the shear panic that consumed me. I was nervous and scared to death. I absolutely hate confrontation. I still do.

We, or I should say, Shelly told everything that happened. She told about every encounter of the abuse. I just sat and nodded my head in agreement. As Granny questioned him about the details Shelly shared, he admitted to everything. He did not try to deny it. He seemed remorseful. He apologize over and over. He wasn't exactly sure why he did the things he did, but that he was a sick individual and would never hurt us again.

I believed that he was sorry and this nightmare was finally over. I was eight, what did I really know. He seemed very convincing. In my own game of "trouble," I finally landed on a six and could get out of home, or so I thought. I guess being the youngest, I was easily manipulated. He continued on with the abuse towards me until I finally had the courage and power to make him stop. I was thirteen.

I never received emotional counseling, and he was never charged with a crime. Life went on as usual. I think my family thought if we would just sweep it under the rug, it would just all go away. The sweeping under the rug approach failed.

Daily, I was tormented with the details of the painful abuse. The feelings, the images, the thoughts wormed their way into my life sometimes on a daily basis. It was like a movie playing over and over in my mind. The effects of years of abuse would create the strategies I used to play the game from here on out. I was defensive, self-protective, isolated, and closed off. I trusted no one, and it was either my way or the highway.

*Not all scars show, not all wounds heal. Sometimes you can't always see the pain someone feels.*—Unknown

On the outside, I appeared to be a typical functioning teenager, but on the inside I was a complete mess: bottling up feelings of fear, depression, worthlessness, guilt, and shame. To keep up with my perfect angel-like appearance, I dated the popular guy in high school. I drank my fair share of Boon's Farm Strawberry Hill and smoked Marlboro Lights just so I could fit in with the cool kids.

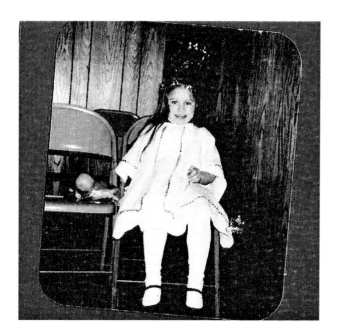

Highland Presbyterian Church Christmas Program, age 5

I played the flute in the marching band until I self-taught myself the basics of piano and joined the pit ensemble in percussion. I sang alto in my high school choir and sang in the All-State Choir for a few years too. I was a Girl Scout and took weekly tap and ballet lessons. I excelled in school, and my love of good grades landed me in the National Honor Society and Beta Club.

I was busy and constantly moving so I did not have to stop and feel the pain. In a valiant effort to cope and mislead people, I put on performances just as I had been trained to do in tap and ballet classes.

Dance Recital, age 8

I gave everyone a first-class performance of whom I wanted to be, or what I thought people wanted to see. I was on a fast-and-furious race to escape what was behind closed doors: a broken home and a stolen childhood. I was on my own little race, only it wasn't so amazing.

Wayne Muller, author of *Sabbath—Finding Rest, Renewal, and Delight in Our Busy Lives*, explains what happens when we run away from things instead of feeling and dealing with what has caused our suffering.

*When we move too fast we shield ourselves from the actual experience of suffering; we see only its outward manifestations and appearances. In our frantic craving for relief, we try to make the appearance of suffering go away. But we risk eradicating the symptoms without ever understanding the disease.*

*We are terrified of the painful grief that is hot to touch, sharp or piercing, so we keep moving, faster and faster, so we will not feel how sad we are, how much we have lost in this life: strength, youthful playfulness, so many friends and lovers, dreams that did not come true, all that have passed away. When we stop even for a moment, we can feel the burning, empty hole in our belly. So we keep moving, afraid the empty fire of loss will consume us.*

In my effort to keep up with a picture perfect life, I did not allow myself to properly deal with the pain of the abuse. I wanted to appear triumphant and strong. I lived a life with a bandage on my heart, not allowing the wound to properly heal. I lived a life just as John Eldredge described.

Although the enemy made it his life's mission to pursue me, I never felt pursued in a healthy way. John Eldredge once said, "It is a rare soul indeed who has been sought after for who she is." So in my pursuit of love and affection, I engaged in meaningless relationships that left me empty and alone.

Most of my young adult life was like a yo-yo—up and down with no particular rhyme or reason. One minute, I was walking closely with God, and the next, I was far away from Him and following my own path. I battled clinical depression and drank alcohol to numb the pain. Nothing ever satisfied the void in my heart. I did whatever humanly possible to keep moving and keep my frail emotions in check.

*God's more interested in where we're heading with Him than all the places we've gone alone.*—Bob Goff

I made my first attempt at playing chess with my teenage cousin Logan. He is highly intelligent and very black and white in his thinking, like me. He is a rule follower and knows many rules in chess. As we were setting up the game, he asked me if I was a defensive player or offensive player. To be honest, I had no idea. What kind of player was I?

He explained that a defensive player's focus is protecting the king and does not take risks of moving higher-value pieces out into the center of the board. An offensive player takes risks. They sacrifice their pieces in order to gain more ground or to capture the higher-value pieces.

As we began to play the game, I was overwhelmed from the start. Which piece is the rook? Which piece is the bishop? How do they move again? Can they move backwards? How can they capture the opponent's piece?

When it was my turn to play, I could not make a move. I had absolutely no idea what piece to move and where to move it to. I was stuck. I would have rather skipped a turn rather than make a wrong move. I can't stand to be wrong.

However, the rules state that every player must make a move whether it is right or it is wrong, and I had to make one regardless. When I tried to move the pawn in a certain direction, Logan would stop me by saying, "No, don't move that one." Then, he would say, "That move will cost you this piece."

After the first few moves of the game were in play, he summed up that I was a defensive player. What, defensive player? I wasn't too fond of his answer. Who really wants to be known as a defensive player, or defensive in their behavior for that matter?

However, the truth was spelled out in black and white right on the board and evident in my reaction to life. Nichole is defensive and a defensive player in life. It's true. I have always vowed to protect myself, to protect my "king." I don't take risks, as that would interfere with my need for control.

Playing the game was too much for me to process; remember this piece, remember that piece, this piece can jump, this one cannot, and this piece cannot move backwards. All I really wanted to do was give up, but I kept playing anyway. He beat me of course. He was better prepared and had more experience playing. However, I learned a valuable lesson that day. You can have all the knowledge you need to play the game, but until you actually play it, it really is of no use.

If you are going to seriously play the game, you are going

to have to stop playing the victim and start playing the victor, as I had to do. I realize how hard opening up is especially when you have deep-rooted trust issues. However, closing yourself off and keeping your pieces tightly knitted together might protect you in the beginning, but eventually it will choke the life out of you. These tiny emotional prisons will cost you your joy and your peace.

So, pick yourself up and dust the emotional dust off as best as you can. It might take many times before you are able to get out of " home," but keep trying. Keep rolling the dice. Keep making the effort. Don't give up right at the starting line. You have a finish line to get to. You have an opponent to capture. Most importantly, you have a game to win.

*She could never go back and make some of the details pretty. All she could do was move forward and make the whole beautiful.*—Terri St. Cloud

# 9 THE POSITION OF PREPARATION

*Fundamental preparation is always effective. Work on those parts of your game that are fundamentally weak.*—Kareem Abdul-Jabbar

After we recover from the effect of the painful first move of the opponent, our pieces should start moving and spreading out across the board towards our opponent. This is

our opportunity to show our opponent the game is far from over and that it is just the beginning. There is nothing more risky than making that first move. It's easy to get caught up in our emotions. We start doubting the move. What have I done? I can't go back now. I've sold the house, I've quit the job, or I've ended the relationship. Fear kicks into overdrive, and we lose our ability to remain calm.

Donald Miller said, "Characters don't really choose to move. They have to be forced. They are probably going to hurt a little, but the story always ends well." I know exactly what he means. I loved playing the victim. It was comforting. It was my right to play this role after all.

Instead of moving out, I did the complete opposite. I closed in. My pieces swarmed in as a means of protection. I was terrified and hell-bent that I would never trust anyone again. At times, I liked being closed off. I felt safe, and it ensured that I had complete control of the game. I was back in the driver's seat and could play the game exactly how I wanted to.

My shyness and my need for isolation often came across as being uptight and rude. My friends and family failed to realize that I was simply protecting myself. I was a fortress; hell-bent on letting no one in so no one could hurt me again. I created myself an internal prison so I could depend on no one but myself.

In borrowing the words from Donald Miller, even though I could feel God leading me to something different, I played the game the way I wanted. It was all about "I, I, and I."

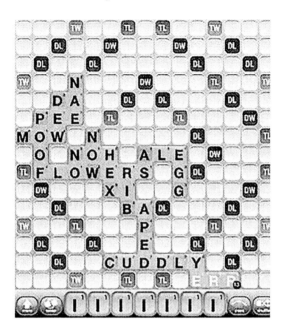

Words with Friends, February 2013

I kept up with this rapid pace as I transitioned from high school into college. Instead of going off to college, I settled on attending my local community college. For the girl who was so desperate to leave home, she sure wasn't going very far. I guess in some weird way, I liked dysfunction. It was "home" to me. It felt safe and it felt comfortable.

My life suddenly changed the first semester of my sophomore year when my boyfriend Todd broke up with me. That heartache led me running miles away to Murray State University that very next semester. While it appeared that I was running away, I was actually positioning myself right where I needed to be. God was realigning my path and that realignment reconnected me with my childhood friend Shelli.

*Sometimes our lives have to be completely shaken up, changed, and rearranged to relocate us to the place we're meant to be.*—Unknown

I met Shelli in the second grade. Shelli, a sweet, curly dark-headed girl, lived with her mom, Malinda, and their little gray-haired poodle, Bootzie. Not only did they live down the street from me, we were classmates in Mrs. Hensley's second-grade class. We became instant friends. We hung out at each other's house, rode our bikes together, and played with other kids in the neighborhood.

Shelli was a gymnast. She was often found wearing her plum-colored "v" neck leotard trimmed in royal blue and running around the yard performing back handsprings. *Show off. Why was she always running around flipping? Couldn't she just walk like the rest of us?*

Sadly, Shelli and her mom moved away to Nashville, Tennessee, when we were in the fourth grade. I lost contact with her until my first day in geology class at Murray State. Standing in the hallway waiting to go in, I saw her. She still looked exactly the same, minus the plum-colored "v" neck leotard.

I couldn't believe we were in class together. It was such an unexpected surprise. We picked up right where we left off like no time had passed. She introduced me to her friends and helped me get adjusted to living on campus. God knew we needed each other. She needed my intellect to pass geology class (yes, she cheated a few times) and I needed to watch her relationship with Christ blossom.

This Divine connection proved to be significant and long lasting through the years that followed. I never learned how to do a backhand spring, but I learned the importance of a relationship with Christ. Shelli introduced me to Joyce Meyer, a loud-mouth female preacher from St. Louis, Missouri.

I remember the very day Shelli first played Joyce's testimony for me. It was on cassette tape. Shelli and I were cruising around Murray in Shelli's mom's coral Volkswagen Rabbit convertible. The top was down and we were blaring the tape. I was hooked from then on out. Joyce's teachings were harsh but effective. She was an open book. She suffered from abuse herself, and she paved the road to freedom and healing for me.

Through the course of our friendship, I watched Shelli's relationship with Christ grow. I watched her establish trust, and I watched her faith develop. Because of her, I learned how to pray and hear from God, but more importantly, I learned not to be ashamed to follow Christ.

We are still friends to this day. Although we are many miles apart, there is no distance in our hearts. She lives in Orlando, Florida, and I am in Nashville, Tennessee. Every year in the fall, we meet up in Gatlinburg, Tennessee, for the Ladies of Legacy retreat. Over forty women gather in a cabin for the weekend to learn about God and deepen the bond that brought us together. We laugh, we cry, and on Saturday night, we have a dance party that concludes with dancing the Electric Slide with Jesus.

Shelli, Ms. Anne (another delightful woman of God), and I at Ladies of Legacy Retreat, Gatlinburg, TN, 2012

Shelli was the catalyst that led me to opening up my life, and little by little, I began moving my pieces out. I began to live again. My desire to play the game was emerging. I was enjoying the relationships from college and beginning to trust people again. I joined a sorority (which I said I would never do) and my friendship base grew and grew. I continued on this path until I found myself relocating to Nashville to complete my internship for graduation.

Several of my classmates had moved to Nashville and were working for a chiropractor as an Exercise Physiologist. They offered me a paying internship. Paying internships were unheard of, so I packed my bags and moved in with my friend Becky, whom I had met in my hometown in Kentucky.

The internship turned into a full-time job, and I worked there about a year before I sensed I needed a change. It's hard for me to be stationary for any given length of time. So, in order to satisfy that need for change, I answered an ad in the paper for store managers for a national grocery store. I worked for the grocery store chain during college so I felt qualified for the position. As my luck turned out, I was offered the management position, and I resigned from my job at the chiropractor's office.

Before being assigned a store to manage, I had to complete a seven-month management training program. While my prior experience got me acclimated to working in a grocery store, managing a store was completely different. During my training program, on average, I spent three to four weeks working in each department—bakery, produce, deli, grocery, meat, and customer service—learning the ropes.

I gathered carts from the parking lot, cashed checks, rang up groceries, unloaded grocery trucks, decorated cakes, baked cookies, sliced deli meat, cut steaks, and made floral arrangements. There was no stone left uncovered. I learned everything. Not only was I training in every department, I was learning my duties of being a store manager—managing people, hiring people, meeting weekly revenue goals, and submitting reports all the while being evaluated by my manager.

The program was intensive and grueling, but I graduated

and was assigned to a store in south Nashville. I was excited. It was my chance to shine and show off my new skills. However, my very first night on the job came with challenges.

It seems we had a drug deal going down in the school supplies aisle. A mother, with her baby in tow, was exchanging a ball of cocaine with another customer. Really, a drug deal in a grocery store? What happened to "cleanup on aisle 6?" This is not what I signed up for and especially on night one. I was 22 years old, a few years out of college, and had absolutely no experience in dealing with drug deals. I certainly did not learn about this during my training program.

My plans to work in a "gravy" store failed miserably. That first night set the tone for the remainder of my time there. A 15-year-old employee stole my car. It took me weeks before I was able to get my car back. A crazy customer threatened to take my life over meat he deliberately let spoil and accused us of selling it to him that way. I was not use to these types of situations. My training store served completely different demographics. The only dilemma we ever faced was running out of eggs and milk.

These types of situations continued during my short career there until exactly two years from my start date, I submitted my letter of resignation. I could not stand the drama and working nights, weekends, and holidays. I wanted a sense of peace and security, and I wanted my life back.

Not really knowing where to go next, I found myself at yet another crossroad, when I decided to move back to Kentucky. My sister had recently given birth to my nephew Trevor so I moved back to help her out with raising him. I thought I could quietly slip back into my old life, in my hometown, and find a good job.

My plan failed. It seemed my resume had fallen into a black hole. I could not find any job in my field and had to accept a temporary position working as a janitor for a local factory. Pushing that garbage can around the factory, in a place that my old friends worked at, embarrassed me. I had left after all. I had gotten my ticket out of this town, but now I found myself right back there only this time I was scrubbing toilets and mopping floors. It seems I was exactly where I needed to be—dealing with my humility issue.

I continued working there for about eight months, when I felt myself being pulled back to Nashville. My sister was adjusting to parenthood quite nicely and really did not need my help. I took a temporary job and slept on my friend Susan's couch until I landed something permanent. Susan was a recruiter for a thriving new and upcoming healthcare company in Franklin, Tennessee and helped me land a job there.

For the next eight years, I climbed my way up the corporate ladder. I took various roles in the company. Each position advanced me both personally and professionally. It was the first time in my life that I was stationary. I was no longer running, and I was building my career and a personal life. I learned more about myself during those eight years than any other time in my life.

I learned what I was capable of and what I was not. I learned how to work with people, problem solve, and improve processes. I developed confidence and discovered my love for teaching and helping others. I was instrumental in building the department I worked in and trained other employees on our software and our processes. This position was where the pieces of my career started fitting together. I liked structure and order. I liked establishing processes and helping others succeed.

*Hardships often prepare ordinary people for an extraordinary destiny.*— C.S. Lewis

In order to establish your position to win the game of life, you've got to go through a period of testing and preparation first. You may have to mop a few floors and scrub a few toilets before you are ready for what God has in store. These years of testing and preparation are like building your resume for God's work to be fulfilled. You need that time of heartache, disappointment, failure, and humility.

As to not give away the entire plot right here, if you took a peek at my resume you would see that my experiences are all over the map. I hop from job to job as I hop around in life. I've worked at Arby's serving Beef N' Cheddars and apple turnovers. I've gathered carts and sliced meat to work my way up from grocery store clerk to store manager. I've mopped floors and scrubbed toilets. I had to experience these jobs so things could be worked out of me: things like pride and self-sufficiency. I also needed these experiences to test my strengths and weakness, build self-confidence, and find my true passions. In the devotion "Passing the Test," Os Hillman explains,

*When God anoints a person, a pattern of testing appears to take place at specific times in their life. God often takes each person through tests to determine if that person will achieve God's ultimate call on his or her life. The person's response to these tests is the deciding factor in whether they can advance to the next level of responsibility in God's Kingdom.*

I believe our tests are different from one another. We might be full of control or bitterness. We might deal with greed or jealousy. We might deal with impatience. We might have a humility issue. So in order to remove those impurities, we have to pass different tests.

We keep encountering these difficulties until we pass, until there is no trace of the impurities. God watches how we respond to the tests too. Will we make an offensive move or a defensive move? Will we respond to the test or will we run from it? We have to pass these tests in order to advance to our next position.

I am grateful for these times of testing and preparation. I learned humility first hand. These times grounded me and molded me into the woman I am today. I believe God prepares us for those worst-case scenarios to ensure we've got what it takes to succeed in what He is calling us to do. I have read that the greater the time of preparation, the greater the calling on our lives.

God may be leading you through a time of preparation and testing. He may have you in a position you literally cannot stand. My advice to you is to allow this process to happen. By working on the areas that are weak, you are growing stronger as an individual. You will be more prepared for what lies ahead and also gain ground against the enemy. You need these experiences to win the game and to fulfill your purpose in life.

*Success is not circumstantial. We usually focus on what we're doing or where we are going, but God's primary concern is who we are becoming in the process. We talk about "doing" the will of God, but the will of God has much more to do with the "being" than "doing." It's not about being in the right place at the right time; it's about being the right person, even if you find yourself in the wrong circumstances.*—Mark Batterson

# 10 THE POSITION OF THE UNKNOWN

*In chess one cannot control everything. Sometimes a game takes an unexpected turn, in which beauty begins to emerge. Both players are always instrumental in this.*—Vladimir Kramnik

We graduate from our times of testing and preparation only to step out into unknown territory. That first step out

into the unknown is terrifying. We have pulled away from what is comfortable, what is safe, and what is secure. We stand there all alone, exposed and vulnerable with no one to protect us. It's is a terrifying feeling. However in order to advance in this game, we need to step out into this unknown territory, take risks, and move our pieces out.

With every move, little by little, my defensive pieces began to move out; leaving me *open* to experience a new life. The walls I crafted began to come down as I eased out into unfamiliar territory. Like the rook, I began craving open spaces.

With my new-found confidence that was birthed during my time at the healthcare company came new dreams and the guts to pursue them. In the fall of 2004, I began attending University of Phoenix Online to pursue my Masters in Education. I had a life-long dream of being a teacher, and I finally decided to pursue it.

Adjusting to school online was challenging. It required discipline. You didn't have to "show up" for class. Online school required that you log on up to 20 hours a week and I already worked a full-time job. Fourteen weeks of class were crammed into three to five short weeks.

I had a hard time understanding the lingo of online school and adjusting to this foreign environment. All communication was done by email in what they call threads, a running list of replies starting with the original response. We were responsible for posting or responding to three to five threads a week in addition to our other course work.

My classmates were scattered all across different time zones and one even lived in Japan. Not only did we have individual assignments, we had group assignments as well. All the different time zones made meeting assignments very challenging. We didn't skype back then, so our primary means of communication was via email. I couldn't just walk up to the teacher with my questions. I had to carefully draft them out in email and hope that point came across. I think my work suffered a little by not having the face-to-face connections, but as time went on, I adjusted.

A few months into graduate school, my friend Amanda and I were having a few drinks and discussing cities we would like to visit. We both really wanted to visit Chicago. I had only visited Chicago once for a day, but I absolutely loved the city.

After a few drinks in, we were back at my house searching the Internet for places to live in Chicago. Somehow, planning our little visit turned into moving. Fortunately, we were both able to transfer with our jobs at the healthcare company. She was a manager and could work remote, and I found a position as a revenue account manager in a hospital in the suburbs of Chicago. Three very short months later, we loaded up our lives and all our belongings in a 27-foot Penske moving truck and we began our new journey.

The move did not go off without a hitch as we had trouble from the start. My house was the last stop as Andrea (our other friend making the move) and Amanda's stuff was already loaded up. We were all packed up and ready to head out, when the back wheel of the Penske fell in the narrow ditch in my neighbor's yard. My friend Ryan was backing the truck out when this happened. We had to call a semi tow truck to move the truck out. This mishap delayed our start by about four hours. I was frustrated from the start.

Maybe I should have taken this misfortune as a sign, but we proceeded ahead anyway. Hours later, we were finally on the road. Andrea led the pack, Amanda brought up the rear, and the Penske and I were sandwiched in between. A fearless trio we were.

I was chosen to drive the Penske because after about a week in Chicago, I would fly back to Nashville for three weeks of new job training. I left my car in Nashville and drove it back to Chicago once the training was complete. I'm not sure I was the best choice. I had no prior truck driving experience. The only experience I had with truck driving is when Shelly and I were kids and we use to play in the cab of J.W.'s truck and talk to other drivers on the CB radio. *Roger, that. Over and Out. What's your 10-4?* It's one of my fond memories as a child.

After a few hours in, I got use to driving the truck. I actually started enjoying it. I was reliving the glory days of my youth. I enjoyed honking the horn at other truck drivers and passing other cars and trucks. I might even have myself a backup career if the account manager job did not work out.

About three hours into the drive, we were cruising right along Interstate 24, when we missed the exit for Interstate 57. This would have led us through Illinois, a path we were familiar with. Instead we found ourselves driving along Interstate 94 through Indiana. Following this unknown path led us straight into road construction, which added a couple more hours to our ever-growing commute. The drive from Nashville to Chicago is roughly 8 hours, and we were close to 13 hours (not including our overnight stop at a hotel).

My nerves began to get the best of me, and I wanted out of the driver's seat (for once). I was over the Penske at this point. It was day two of moving and I was still in my clothes from the day before. My overnight bag full of fresh clothes and toiletries was mistakenly packed early on in the truck. I felt gross and irritable. All I wanted was a hot shower, fresh clothes, and my own bed.

After many more miles of tense driving, we arrived into

Chicago. We were greeted by thousands of runners who were participating in the Chicago Marathon. Just our luck, our new high-rise apartment was positioned right on the eighth mile of the course.

With my nerves rattling, I somehow maneuvered the truck down Local Lake Shore Drive, dodged the excited runners, and was minutes away from my destination when I had a breakdown. In order to get to our new home on Melrose Avenue, we had to turn down Belmont Avenue, which was one street over. There was a small overpass at the beginning of Belmont Avenue. For fear that the Penske would not clear the overpass (I think the clearance was near 12 ft.), I turned back on Local Lake Shore Drive and headed to the next exit, Irving Park. I panicked. I was not thinking clearly.

I thought Amanda would follow behind me, but for some reason she did not. She kept following Andrea. I had no idea where I was going. I pulled off the next exit about two miles up the road which sat parallel to Lake Michigan. I threw the truck into park and wept. Roughly twenty minutes later, I calmed down, got in touch with Andrea, and she came to find me.

I would rather abandon the truck and all of our belongings than get back behind the wheel again. I wanted nothing more to do with that truck. However, after a few minutes pep-talk, Andrea convinced me to get back in the Penske and drive home. I was inches away from the finish line. After all, I was the logical choice to drive the truck with all my most recent experience.

Ten short minutes later, the Penske was parked right in front of our new apartment. I finally reached my long overdue destination. I was never so glad to be there. I could finally shower and change into new clothes. I could properly brush my teeth and hair.

Thankfully, we had friends and Andrea's and Amanda's parents awaiting our arrival. They created an assembly line and quickly moved all our belongings into our new 14th floor apartment. Three hours later we were all settled in.

After settling into my new surroundings and my new position at work, I began to explore the city. Learning how to navigate this large city brought many challenges. In an attempt to catch the bus, I would always find myself on the wrong side of the street and would end up in less than desired locations. Public transportation was not my friend, so I decided to travel mainly by foot.

I equipped myself with my Streetwise Chicago map and off I went exploring. There were days I would grab a coffee from Starbucks and head west. I had no agenda or set destination. I was just exploring and taking in the sights. I'll never forget the day I discovered there was a Wendy's directly near the Target on Addison Street. I loved Wendy's as much and I loved Target. I was finally finding my way.

Everything was so new. I had to establish my bank, find grocery stores, places to shop and eat. I got lost many times, but eventually I learned my way around the city and felt at home. I decided to give public transportation another try as Amanda and I were off in search of NY & Co (our favorite clothing store). We searched the Internet and the only store we could find was way out in the Western Suburbs near Midway Airport. We were desperate for fashion so we went anyway.

First, we could catch the Red Line on the E.L. (elevated train) and head downtown on the Dan Ryan. Then, we had to transfer to the Orange Line to Midway (airport), and then catch the bus that would take us to the shopping mall. It all seemed worth it in our minds.

A couple of stops on the Red Line, a delusional-acting man jumped on the train and started yelling, "The train is on fire, the train is on fire, get off now!" It could have been my paranoia setting in, but I swore I smelt rubber burning. Deciding to play it cool, we agreed that it was best to slip off the train as if this was our stop. Not knowing where to go next, we headed upstairs and started walking in a random direction.

Much to our surprise, we discovered that we were near

State Street in downtown Chicago. A few blocks later, we stumbled upon NY & Co, Old Navy, Nordstrom Rack, and H & M. It felt as if we had hit the shopping jackpot.

In those two short years I lived in Chicago, I fell madly in love with the city. I met my amazing friends Betsy, Emily, Rosie, Lisa, Sara, Carolyn, Chuck, Ally, Jesse, and Dave. I felt alive. I found an appetite for life. I visited and explored every square mile of the city.

I went to museums and Cubs games; I sat atop of the John Hancock building and sipped martinis while enjoying the view. I went to street fairs in various neighborhoods. On Sunday afternoons, my friend Lisa and I would ride our bikes down the path along Lake Michigan down to Navy Pier so we could grab a hot dog and a Coke. I experienced some of the most joy-filled days of my life there.

However, after living the big city life close to two years, I felt my heartstrings tugging and calling me back home. I was wrapping up graduate school and it was time for me to student teach. I really wanted to teach in a school similar to an environment I grew up in—a small town. I was also ready to settle down and plant some roots. I had just turned 30 years old.

In looking back, I never had any regrets about leaving Chicago. Chicago brought me to life. It's where I found my appetite for life. I lived and I lived well during this chapter of my life. If I had never moved to Chicago, I would have never lived in the building where the movie *The Breakup* with Jennifer Aniston and Vince Vaughn was filmed. They filmed some of the scenes in apartment 9B.

Filming notice for the movie *The Break Up*

I would have never completed my first half-marathon in Chicago with my childhood best friend. We still run half-marathons to this day.

Angie and I, Chicago Half-Marathon 2006

I would never have had the opportunity to see Oprah. Well, we had to settle for a glimpse of the exterior of her studios.

My cousin Shelly and I posing at Harpo Studios, Chicago, IL

I would have never met my amazing friends and had all those amazing experiences with them had I not stepped out into the unknown. I am so grateful that I did.

Sometimes life takes an unexpected turn and our plans get derailed. Sometimes we miss the exit altogether. It is during these unknown times of life is where we find our place in this world and the beauty of life truly begins.

Don't be afraid to step out. Don't be afraid to hop off the train or take the wrong bus. You will find your place again. If you make a wrong turn, you will still end up in the right place. It might just take you a few extra steps, but God's grace will always meet you right where you are at and get you back where you need to be. I promise.

*Never be afraid to trust an unknown future to a known God.*—Corrie Ten Boom

# PHASE TWO: THE MIDDLE GAME:

## *The Attack*

# 11 THE BLOCKED POSITION

*In the game of life, it's a good idea to have a few early losses, which relieves you of the pressure of trying to maintain an undefeated season.—* Bill Vaughan

According to the article "The Three Phases of a Chess Game," after the first 8 to 12 moves have been completed, it's time to transition to the middle phase of the game. The

middle phase is the time to seize the opportunity to stabilize or cripple your opponent and break down his defenses around his king. When you get your opponent frustrated and overwhelmed, you can take him out of the game. Some tactics for breaking down your opponent are to

- simply make your opponent weak and distracted.
- protect your king, but don't make that your primary focus.
- pressure your opponent into moves that will enable you to attack later.
- trade your pieces if possible.

I settled back into Nashville, planted roots, and bought a townhouse. During the day, I student taught at a small rural elementary school in Williamson County, just as I hoped for, and at night I settled back into my previous position at the corporate office at the healthcare company. Around the time I was wrapping up student teaching, an opportunity for a permanent fifth-grade position opened up at that school. The only thing standing in my way of this opportunity was my teaching license.

In order to obtain my license, I had to pass the National Board Exams otherwise known as the Praxis Exams. I had to pass four of them. As it turned out, I passed three exams and failed one. I failed that one exam twice and each time by one point. *One* point blocked me from a permanent teaching position. I was crushed.

I continued on with my job, which resumed back to days, and at night I studied for that final Praxis exam. A few months later, I crossed paths with my hometown boyfriend, Mike. We'd lost touch for many years and reconnected on MySpace. He was single, I was single, and so it felt natural to pick up where we had left off. He was crazy and chaotic, and I loved him deeply. He made me laugh, and he made me feel special. So, without much hesitation, I dove right back into this old and familiar relationship (I hope you see the pattern forming here.)

My cousin Shelly and her husband Brad had started attending a church in Clarksville, Tennessee. One of their closest friends had decided to start his own church. It was just the place I was looking for—a new beginning and a place to fit in. Secretly, I wanted Mike to start attending church with me. It seemed like the best solution for all parties involved.

The church was a modern-day miracle. The pastor received two million dollars in cash from a wealthy donor from Texas. The church would be debt free from the start. People began relocating to help plant the church. It was an exciting time for us.

This was a time for my dreams to be birthed as well. I always felt burdened to help women. I'm sure it stemmed from my painful childhood. Out of that desire to help women, I started a Women's Ministry called *The Oaks* for the Oaks of Righteousness based on Isaiah 61:3. *They will be called oaks of righteousness, a planting of the LORD for the display of his splendor.* Shelly created this card to advertise the study I was going to teach. Seeing my dreams manifested in print was surreal.

For eleven weeks, thirteen women and I met every Thursday to take part in Beth Moore's *Breaking Free* Bible study. It seemed as if the church plant was taking off as well. My friend Lisa and I started Operation Blessings. We created a clothes closet, and we collected and recycled cans so we could use the money for trips or blessing others. The church was growing rapidly and we were changing people's lives. It was a wonderful time in my life.

Eventually, that all changed. The preacher had his own demons to deal with, and his appetite for power and control got the best of him. I fell for many of his lies. The preacher's wife battled with her own insecurities and felt left out in the work I was doing. In order to pacify her feelings, he strongly suggested that I take a back-seat role in the ministry, and so I did.

Later on down the road, the congregation learned that our tithes and offerings were used for individual purposes and not for the church or its people. Our campaign to pave the parking lot funded trips out of state and a brand new Hummer. We were funding an extravagant lifestyle instead of God's kingdom.

I remember the night clearly, the night I decided to walk away from the church. My mom and I sat up until 3 a.m. talking and weighing over the pros and cons of leaving. The next day, I went to church, paid my final tithes to them, and walked out the door. My relationship with Mike started fading too. We both wanted different things so we decided to end the relationship. I found myself again starting over again in more ways than one.

*There are far better things ahead than any we leave behind.*—C.S. Lewis

In the fall of 2009, my boyfriend at the time, Steve, and I were traveling back to Nashville from a wedding in Charleston, South Carolina. We had just passed through Asheville, North Carolina, and were about an hour away from

Knoxville, Tennessee, when I noticed an overhead sign urging motorists to turn around. Steve was driving and proceeded to ignore the sign (typical man). We were forced to exit the highway at the Strawberry Plains exit and were greeted by the highway patrol. They informed us that a massive rockslide was just ahead. The rockslide spilled over both sides of the interstate making it impassable.

Photo credit: http://www.ncdot.gov/travel/i40_rockslide/

Forced to turn back to Asheville, we had to travel towards Bristol, Tennessee. This added a few more hours to our already extensive road trip. I was pretty upset at first. The sign kept telling Steve to turn around, and he simply ignored it. I was tired from the busy weekend at the wedding, and we just added four more hours to our drive. I simply wanted to get home and sleep in my own bed.

We would have had to take a detour regardless as there was no other way around the rockslide. I could either sit and stew in my frustration, or I could enjoy the ride. Steve told a few jokes to lighten my mood and eventually I gave in. I decided to let go of my frustration and enjoy the ride. The unexpected interruption led us through a different side of the Appalachian Mountains, a side I had never seen before. The foliage was beautiful. The trees were saturated in thick green, yellow, orange, and red leaves. It was absolutely beautiful.

Sometimes roadblocks happen in life. We are cruising right along enjoying the view, when we reach a place we cannot pass. We are forced to turn around and seek an alternate course. Maybe the blocked position was a means to protect us from what was ahead. Maybe the blocked position prevented us from heading in the wrong direction. In the devotion "A Talking Donkey," Os Hillman explains his reasoning on blocked positions,

> There are times when pushing harder, trying to manipulate the circumstance, or pressing those around you is not the response to have to the roadblock. God may be trying to have you reconsider your ways. God may be doing one of four things when you are faced with an obstacle: 1) He's blocking it to protect you. 2) His timing to complete this stage is not the same as yours, and He may need you to go through a process of character refinement. 3) He may want other players to get in place, and the circumstances are not yet ready for them to enter. 4) He may be using the process to develop patience in you. Relying on the Holy Spirit to know which one applies to your situation is the key to moving in God's timing.

God has an aerial view that we do not have the ability to see. He knows exactly what lies ahead and what turns we need to take. He will block any move that is needed to change our course of direction. You may come to the end of your path and find that you cannot go any further and be forced to turn around in the opposite direction. You may miss the perfect opportunity for one small misstep. You may find that people are not who they say they are and you may have to walk away from the relationship.

Whatever the situation, God knows what is best for you. He knows what direction you should travel and how your life will turn out. All you have to do is trust Him, take the path before you, and continue playing the game.

*If the path before you is clear, you're probably on someone else's.—* Joseph Campbell

# 12 THE POSITION OF RISK

*Play the game for more than you can afford to lose, only then will you learn the game.*—Winston Churchill

In May 2006, my sorority sister and good friend, Renah, got married in Jamaica. There was a big group of us attending the wedding, so we rented three large houses to accommodate all of us. Since so many of us were traveling a

great distance for the wedding, she encouraged us to treat the trip like a vacation as well. One of the activities she planned for our group was to go zip lining. I wanted to go, but I was/am deathly afraid of heights.

One jolting bus ride up a mountain, 45 minutes later, I found myself strapped into a harness, secured with a helmet, and hosed down in bug spray. After a quick orientation, where I sobbed the whole time, I was ready to make my first jump. The first couple of jumps did not go off without a hitch. I screamed and cried the entire length of each jump. "I can't do it," I cried. One jump was 25 feet long. My friends were thoroughly enjoying themselves, but I could not pull myself together.

By the time I had reached the third platform, something changed inside. My crying turned to laughter, and I sensed that the cable holding me was safe and secure. I decided to "let go" emotionally and enjoy the ride, which I did 13 more times.

To prove that my enjoyment was real, I raced ahead of my friends so I could be the first to jump off. *Look at me, I'm so daring. I'm not afraid anymore.* I was acting like a show off, flipping around like my friend Shelli, minus the plum-colored "v" neck leotard trimmed in royal blue. It was so freeing and so exhilarating. I loved every minute of the experience. It is much like a life with God if we would simply trust that His "cable" would sustain us.

Zip lining in Jamaica, 2006

Robert McKee once said, "Humans naturally seek comfort and stability. Without an inciting incident that disrupts their comfort, they won't enter into a story. They have to get fired from their job, sign up for a marathon, purchase a ring, or sell their house. The character has to jump into the story, into the discomfort and the fear, otherwise the story will never happen."

When I accepted the fifth-grade teaching position in a school in Clarksville, after a 20-minute phone interview, I jumped into my next position—risk. The doubt began to sink in. Should I leave a job that I've worked at for over eight years for one I am uncertain of? Will my house sell? Am I qualified to teach? How am I going to make this work?

I had so many questions and so many emotions running inside of me. Maybe I should have taken what happened at the church in Clarksville as a sign that the door to that town was closed, but my desire to teach simply outweighed it. After all, I had finally passed that final Praxis exam and landed a fifth-grade teaching position. It seems this position was the reason the other fifth-grade teaching position was blocked.

It seemed as if my dreams were finally coming true. I was

a first-year teacher with high hopes and dreams of impacting children. My childhood created in me an obligation that I felt for children, and I wanted to make a difference in their lives. I prayed for a successful school year, and for God to hand-select the children He wanted in my classroom. Be careful what you pray for <insert smiley face>.

The students' ages ranged from 10 to 13 years old. The students came from every socioeconomic class and race. They had their share of weaknesses and dreams as wide as the ocean. They wanted to be professional athletes, writers, artists, fashion designers, and rappers, and I would be the one to foster those dreams.

The dynamics between the children changed from one day to the next. One minute they were best friends and the next they were enemies. I was often teased by my colleagues for the many times I rearranged my classroom. Every few weeks, I was separating students and rearranging desks, only to find them best friends again. It was exhausting and frustrating. The only thing they had in common was a strong desire to be accepted and loved. I shared that special bond with them.

Every day presented a challenge. My house was still on the market and gas was up to $4.00 a gallon. I was carrying unwanted stress that found ways to trickle in and out of my day. To try and compensate for the financial strain of an hour and a half commute each way from Nashville to Clarksville, I stayed with my close friend Amy and her family a few nights a week. Living out of a suitcase only added to my frustration. My home was my sanctuary, my place of comfort, and I was not fond of leaving my place of comfort.

The school was in a military town, and the students came and went with no rhyme or reason. The parents who served in the military might be transferred to another base in the middle of the year, or parents who were deployed might come home on leave and pull their kids out for a two-week trip to Disney World. I never knew how long the students were going to stay or when they would leave. I had to quickly adapt to constant change.

I was immediately overwhelmed. I never felt that I was capable of meeting the demands and responsibilities of teaching. Lesson plans were to be turned in weekly for evaluation. Planning for instruction was so involved it crept into my personal time. Days and nights ran together. Weekends were consumed with grading papers or the other administrative tasks that I was responsible for. I never had ample time to relax and regroup from the previous week.

There was so much emphasis on student performance, that I took it personally if my students failed to meet their learning expectations. It took all my emotional strength to combat the issues in the classroom and left little room for teaching. There were days I cried more than I laughed. I was exhausted physically and emotionally.

I never realized how children were affected by poverty. Sometimes school would be the only place that a child might get something to eat. The school sent them home with fuel packs on Friday to try and sustain them over the weekend. Some of my students were neglected and filthy; baths were few and far between. Fortunately, we had a shower in the school and plenty of clean clothes we could provide them. These conditions were heartbreaking.

I had emotionally distraught children who thought violence could solve any dispute. Scissors and pencils served many purposes; instruments to aid in education were also tools for self-defense. If I had my back turned for one second, all chaos would erupt. I broke up fights, counseled, wiped tears, and loved unconditionally; all the while neglecting myself. I was pushing myself to the extreme and not getting the help I needed.

*Experience is a hard teacher because she gives the test first, the lesson afterwards.*—Unknown

During my time at the school, God gave me a friend who I will refer to as "Sandpaper." She was a teacher's aide at the school. At times, she could be rough and abrasive, but she was good for smoothing out the "rough spots" in people's lives. I met her the first day we reported to school. My first encounter with her was during team-building activities. She was the captain of my group. She was busy barking out orders on how to complete the task: have all members stand on a tablecloth and successfully turn it over without using our hands and not stepping off the tablecloth. Our team lost, which she was not pleased with. Hoping this would be my last encounter with her did not work out either. She was the hall monitor on my floor.

Every morning she would peek her head in the doorway and yell (seriously yell), "Good morning Ms. Cornelius!" I would look up from my laptop, quickly respond, and then go back to working. I kept thinking, "Please go away!" "Why won't she take the hint?" This just proves that God knows what is best for us, and He has some serious jokes.

A few weeks later, some friends and I were going to the Joyce Meyer Women's Convention in St. Louis, Missouri. We were walking around checking out the exhibits, when much to my surprise, there she was. Out of 20,000 plus women, I ran into "Sandpaper." How on Earth did this happen? We were in a city hundreds of miles away from home and in an arena packed with thousands of women, and I ran into her. Never underestimate the power of God and His desire to make a connection.

I finally gave in and began pursuing a friendship with her, a friendship that proved to be a blessing. We talked every morning sharing our hearts for God and our struggles in life. It seems we had more in common than I realized. That *unlikely* friendship sealed with Christ proved to be very rewarding and sustained me for the months ahead.

"Sandpaper" and I pictured at Fudpuckers in Destin, FL, 2009

Thinking the days at the church in Clarksville were long behind me, proved to be wrong. When I walked out the door that last day, I never expected to hear from that pastor again. In the middle of February, I stopped at a random book store in search of a new daily devotion. I was in need of something to help me cope to my new life as a teacher. Randomly, I picked up Joyce Meyer's *New Day, New You* and began thumbing through the pages. Someone had stuck a postcard advertising services at a local church.

I picked up the card to read it and realized that it belonged to my previous church. *What? How did this happen?* I looked around for cameras and a team of people from Candid Camera to come out of hiding, but they did not.

I purchased the devotion and took the card with me. Apparently, I needed some closure in this situation. Although I forgave the situation and the people associated with the church, I never had a face to face conversation with the pastor. With a little help and encouragement from my cousin Shelly, I called the pastor and we decided to meet up for coffee.

We met at Starbucks and the situation was not as painful as I had imagined. We both shared our hearts and I told him that I forgave him. You could see the relief on his face when I uttered those words. We parted ways, and I never had a desire to reach out to him again. That part of the chapter was closed. I made my peace with the situation and could finally move on.

What I learned during this time and the time spent at this church is people are going to hurt you, even Christians. The Church is not a guaranteed safety zone. Also, I cannot put my faith in man alone.

If you have been hurt by organized religion, I am deeply sorry. I know that pain you have felt or are feeling. It took me a great deal of time to move past this situation and to trust the "Church" again. However, I do know that there are many wonderful churches out there filled with wonderful people, grace, and love. God will lead you to a safe place, a place where you can grow and let your heart heal. I know this, because He did this for me.

Part of taking risks in the game of life involves opening ourselves up to new experiences and the possibility of getting hurt. It is the risks that we take that "open" us up and move us forward. Don't regret taking this risk and don't stop taking risks altogether. The pain is only temporary. You will see why this piece was vital for you to reach your place of promise.

*Life experience is what defines our character, even if it means getting your heart broken or being lied to. You know, you need the downs to appreciate the ups. Going on the adventure or taking that risk is important.— Nev Schulma*

# 13 THE POSITION OF DEFEAT

*You can't win unless you learn how to lose.*—Kareem Abdul-Jabbar

With the first two nine weeks and Christmas break behind me, the third nine weeks was in full swing and spring break was approaching fast. I seemed to have found my rhythm as a teacher. I received promising feedback on my first two teacher evaluations, and the end of the school year

was in sight. It seemed I was going to make it after all, or so I thought.

On this particular day in March, I was told one of the students in my class had a gun in his backpack. This was not the first time I was faced with a weapon in my classroom. I had one student who brought in a BB gun with the intentions of shooting another student in the knee. I was rattled and the stress set the tone for my day.

No number of textbooks or amount of practical experience prepared me for what lay ahead. I was stretched and pulled in so many different directions and the pressure made me collapse. I was overloaded both mentally and physically. My emotions got the best of me and caused me to make a costly decision. I just needed some form of release.

After a morning of gun searches and investigating the accusation, my classroom was unruly and out of control, and one student in particular was feeding off the chaos. This child struggled often with his work, so, he compensated for his struggles by being the class clown. On that day, he was putting on a little show.

His performance to the class added to my rattled nerves. I had asked him several times to remove his math project from the trash, but he refused. He was being disrespectful with his words and disobedient with his actions. Frustrated and angry, I erupted. I was not thinking clearly, and I did not choose my words wisely. I told the student to get his "damn stuff and go to time out."

As the words started rolling off my tongue, I knew the outcome was not good, but the release of the stress *far* outweighed my concern. My new-found comfort did not last long as my mind raced with fears of what lay ahead. What would the student say to his parents? How would they react? Would I be suspended or even lose my job? These questions tormented my mind. I was absolutely terrified. My first reaction was to run away, but I decided to return to school the next day and face the consequences, as painful as they may be.

111

As soon as the students started arriving the next day, they were pulled into the principal's office for questioning about what they witnessed the day before. Each student was honest with his or her answers. After all, honesty was a trait that I did my best to instill in them, and I expected no less from them and especially myself.

When they returned back to class, they were pretty upset. They were afraid I was going to lose my job. I praised them for their honesty and explained why my actions were wrong. However, I was afraid of the same thing. It seems I failed them and failed myself.

Next, I was called to the principal's office to meet with administration and the student's mother. I did my best to keep my composure and explain my reactions to the events that led up to the incident with the student. Trying to explain the reason for using a word of profanity toward a student is not easily accepted, nor should it be.

No amount of apologies or expressed regret eased the tension or diffused the heightened emotions. *One* word tarnished my reputation, my credibility, and my integrity— aspects of my life that I spent years perfecting. It was as if the enemy had played the old "Pirc/Modern" move to ruin my reputation.

The fact that I loved my students and did my best no longer mattered. According to the administration, I was a professional and should have acted like one. The gun scare was early in the morning and the incident with the student was toward the end of the day. That was an ample amount of time, according to them, to recover and was no excuse for my behavior.

The evidence was stacked against me and there was nothing else to do, but be accountable. My contract for the next year was not renewed as a result of my actions. As a result of the incident, it was decided by the administration that the student be moved into another classroom. I was advised to make little or no contact with him in order for the child to successfully complete the school year.

After the shock wore off, my classroom went back to normal; the only difference was that there was always someone looking over my shoulder. I had to teach with my door open at all times. I desperately wanted to escape, but deep down I knew that I needed to finish out my contract with dignity.

*Please know that often what feels like the end of the world is simply a challenging pathway to a far better place.*—Karen Salmansohn

Spring break finally arrived, which was just the change I needed. I headed to Fort Walton Beach, Florida with my teacher friend, Angie. Her parents lived there and we were able to stay with them for the week. I spent the week relaxing at the beach and reading books. I let the comfort of the ocean soothe my troubled mind.

Feeling recharged and restored, I set out to complete the school year under the radar. My plans of making it through the last couple months of the school year with ease took a slight detour in the beginning of May. This particular Sunday morning, I woke up with intense pain in my abdomen. It felt as if my stomach was on fire. I am stubborn and would rather self-diagnose myself as opposed to going to the doctor, so I assumed the pain would ease up and decided to go to work the next day.

That next morning I could barely stand up straight as I was doubled over in pain. The teacher next door was very concerned and convinced me to go to the hospital. I dropped my kids off at lunch and drove myself to the hospital. A few short hours later, I was being wheeled to surgery. My appendix was rupturing. I immediately called "Sandpaper," and she rushed to the hospital and stayed with me until my mom and grandmother arrived.

What was supposed to be a simple surgery with a quick recovery led to some of the darkest days of my life. It seems my surgeon failed to remove my entire appendix and the residuals became infected. I was so sick and dehydrated that I lost twelve pounds in four days. I could not make the drive back to Nashville so I stayed with my Aunt Judy in Kentucky. For nearly seven days, I lay in bed with barely any physical strength to move. At times, I did not think I was going to make it as I was tormented with thoughts of regret, mental anguish, and self-hate.

*Though I fall, I will rise again.*—Micah 7:8

If you watched Super Bowl XLVII on February 3, 2013, you witnessed the San Francisco 49ers receive a surge of power that changed the game. Chris Miller from WWL First News said, "It may go down in history as 'The Blackout Bowl.' A power surge early in the third quarter knocked out half the lights in the Superdome, and it took more than half an hour to resume the game. And when the lights came back on, so did the San Francisco 49ers, pulling within a touchdown of winning before ultimately losing to the Baltimore Ravens, 34–31."

By the grace of God, I received a surge of power and made it through the end of the school year. My power ran out the day I opened my mouth and uttered that one word, but God took over the day I answered the call of the alarm clock and got out of bed.

After a two-week medical leave, I returned to school to finish out what was left of the school year. By showing up, I laid the rumors to rest that I was dead, at least that is what my kids were spreading around school. Twelve pounds lighter, and grayish in color, I did appear to be half dead, but in reality, I was not.

I finished up the school year. I boxed up my personal things, cleaned up my classroom, and said my final goodbyes; at last, this part of the journey was over. This was a bittersweet time for me. It was a year of tremendous growth and struggle. For that, I have never been the same.

I wrote in my journal a thank-you note to God. I thanked Him for this time, a time to see who I truly was and a time to be loved by kids who simply longed for love themselves. They were the *heartbeat* to a new journey I would soon find myself on.

A sweet, red-headed, freckled-face student drew me a report card and gave it to me on the last day of school. In his eyes, I had passed the year with an A plus and was ready to go on to the next year. The fun times in the classroom and times spent outside playing dodge ball convinced him that I was the best teacher he ever had.

Ink cannot convey what that little boy and his report card did for me. Despite all the mistakes I made, he said that I was the best teacher ever. No enemy can ever steal that moment of joy.

*Before Alice got to Wonderland, she had to fall pretty hard down a deep hole.—Unknown*

On a random Saturday evening in the fall, some friends and I gathered together for game night. Jenga was our game of choice for the evening. It was my first time and quite possibly my last time playing this game. The pieces were assembled to create the tower, and it was time for player number one to make a play.

We took turns, man, woman, man, woman. The men would tease or make a comment like, "Oh, don't move that one!" or yell out "It's about to fall!" to add a little intensity to the game—a likely strategy of any opponent. There were the brave ones who made risky moves, and then there were the ones who played it safe, like me, who chose the safest piece, the piece in the middle, to move.

When my turn arrived, my heart began to beat out of my chest. My hands were sweaty, and I hesitated to move. It was as if I was playing chess for the first time. Of course, my lack of movement led to my friends making fun of me, which led to further anxiety. It was a game, but I took it seriously just as I do any aspect of my life.

What if I made the wrong move? What if the tower fell on

my turn? What if? What if? It would be my fault and everyone would be upset with me. As a result, the tower fell and crumbled onto the ground. No one was mad either. They just laughed as I carried on and on. They helped me re-assemble the tower so we could play again, which I did several more times.

*Unless the Lord protects a city, guarding it with sentries will do no good.*—Psalm 127:1

From the outside, towers appear to be strong and engineered against destruction. We fail to look at them from the inside. On the outside we are smiling, but on the inside we are a mess. It's hard to tell what is going on until everything falls apart. I too have crumbled just like the tower in Jenga. Everything from my reputation, character, and security collapsed in one brief moment, and I was left with an overwhelming mess to sift through. Life changed instantly.

When I look back to the chess game I played with my cousin Logan, I think about that little pawn that I moved out to the center of the board in an effort to take a risk. It was out there all alone with no other pieces to protect it. I wanted to move it back to safety, but the rules of the game would not allow it. Moving it forward caused greater risk of capture so I kept it there.

All the pawn wanted to do was take some chances, live out dreams, but it quickly found itself in defeat. It seems defeat was an important part of the journey. What I have learned through this experience is that defeat is often temporary. The game is far from over. If you find yourself in defeat, it might be time to sit out for a while, rest, and build your strength so you can get back in the game and take down that opponent.

*Never let a stumble in the road be the end of the journey.*—Unknown

# 14 THE POSITION OF ENCAMPMENT

*My problem with chess was that all my pieces wanted to end the game as soon as possible.*—Dave Barry

It took about six weeks before I recovered physically, recovering mentally was a whole other challenge. During my time of recovery, I logged many hours on the couch which

led me to depression. Confined to the couch with just my thoughts, the enemy had prime real estate in my mind as he had more control of the board. He took advantage of my defenseless position.

Satan tormented me with thoughts of regret, guilt, and failure. He tried to convince me that I was a monster and should never be allowed to work with children again. I believed him. I started to question God in all of this. If He can control the wind and the seas with His commands, couldn't He have turned this situation around? I appealed my case with the teachers' union, but they did not side with me. I fervently prayed, begged, and pleaded that God would help overturn the decision to not renew my contract. Why didn't He?

*Trust always requires some unanswered questions in your life.*—Joyce Meyer

Those thoughts and unanswered questions led to self-hatred and even thoughts of suicide. Lying there deep into depression, I begged and pleaded with God to let me die. I saw no hope for the future. The pain and the mental anguish were far greater than any strength remaining in me (Psalm 13:1-2). I lost all glimmer of hope.

Luckily, I was surrounded with a good defense. I was enclosed with prayer warriors. I prayed, family prayed, and friends prayed. Every day and sometimes every moment, I had to fight through the negativity, the voices telling me I was a monster, and that I did not matter. Little by little, I fought my way out of the darkness. I found my hope again.

*The decision to press on with God instead of accepting defeat shows the world our true identity—a heart after God.*—John Eldredge

I grew up in Kentucky, the Bluegrass state. I grew up watching Kentucky basketball and the Kentucky Derby. It was a Kentucky tradition. It was always a dream of mine to go to the Derby. It just so happened that my friend Mina had an extra ticket for a seat in the grandstand. I debated the cost, but decided the experience would be worth the money. So, I bought a fancy hat and dress and set off for the Run for the Roses.

KY Derby May – Churchill Downs 2011

I read my program, studied the horses, and placed my $2 bet on my favorite horse. I was a bit skittish with my bet and decided to play it safe. Even though I was a bit gun-shy, I was still aiming for the great trifecta. A trifecta win is a bet where the bettor predicts which horse will come in first, second, and third places in that exact order which will leave you a very wealthy person. As it turned out, I did not win the great trifecta; however, I took home a few dollars and new memories.

In my own life and current situation, the enemy placed the right bet and won the great trifecta. I was in the process of mending my heart from the failed experience at the church, coming to terms that the job I loved was over, and healing both physically and mentally. My life came to a complete halt without my permission and I was not ok with it. My "piece" was not moving. In chess, this position is called stalemate.

Legally, the player cannot make any move and the game ends in a draw: no winner and no loser. Luckily for me, this position was not permanent. Donald Miller said, "The greatest stories are the ones in which the character's life is at stake. There needs to be a question as to whether the character will make it, whether he will defeat the enemy or the enemy will defeat him." In my current position, I questioned whether I would survive this ordeal or not. Could I overcome this and find my joy again?

*They abode in their places in the camp till they were whole.*—Unknown

When I was a young child, every weekend my family would go camping at Kentucky Lake. Aunts, uncles, cousins, parents, and grandparents would load up the campers and hitch the boats and make the 45-minute journey to the lake. We camped out right at the base of the Kentucky Lake Bridge. We had instant access to the lake.

I loved camping, building a fire, riding in the boat, water skiing, swimming, and riding the moped around the camp grounds. I was young, free, and on an adventure. I was away from the woes of the world for a little bit. Camping was not always as glamorous as I described. You had to sleep on the hard ground, you had to fight off pesky bugs, and you had to use gross and stinky facilities. However, I kept going back every weekend because I simply loved camping. A few less than desired conditions were well worth the experience.

*Don't waste the season of life you are in now because you want the next one to come.*—Unknown

When Shelly's third child Cooper was born, she made her grand entrance five weeks early. Her early arrival came with several complications. She was admitted to Vanderbilt Children's Hospital in Nashville, Tennessee so they could regulate her temperature and body weight. In the photo, the little nugget I am holding was just five days old when she was admitted to the hospital.

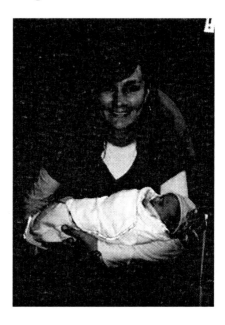

For days on end, she camped out in an incubator or what I like to call "Cooper's Condo." It seemed unfair to have this new budding life boxed in away from the world. On the outside she seemed perfectly fine, but it seemed her insides needed a little more care. She needed a place to heal.

Friends and family camped out right along with her. We waited, and we prayed for her temperature to raise back to normal. We had waited nine long months, or rather seven months and three weeks, for her to join us, and we couldn't even get our arms around her.

Like Cooper, I found myself in a new position—encampment—and had to camp out for a while. I camped out in my condo and couldn't leave. I didn't have the means or the strength to do so. My companions, depression, self-loathing, and heartache, were hanging out for support. They wanted me to stay in my condo indefinitely.

This was not the kind of camping I signed up for. This

form of camping did not provide me any sense of freedom like I experienced at Kentucky Lake. I actually felt like I was in prison. Holly Gerth described the season of encampment in a passage in *You're Already Amazing.*

*There are many reasons why God may tell us to "encamp" for a period of time. For the Israelites, it was an extended "time out" because they blatantly rebelled against God. But that is not always the case. God may have us "encamp" because we are weary, we need to heal, or we are being prepared for what lies ahead.*

For myself, I was camping out because: one, my mind and body needed to heal, and two, I was being prepared for what lay ahead. Holly said, "Whatever reason you feel 'encamped' in your life right now, use this time to rest and receive the truth your heart needs for the journey." Like little Cooper, on the outside you appear fine, but you might just need to hang out in the condo for a little while and rest before it is time to pack up and get moving again.

Pastor Denny Livingston said that in order to face the Battle of Jericho, the battle right before crossing over into the Promised Land, you have to sit out a while, rest, and heal your wounds. Once you are ready, you can start marching around the walls of Jericho and take your place of Promise. My place of promise was on the horizon and I needed this time to rest and heal.

As time went on, my health began to improve, so it seemed natural that my career would be on the upswing as well. Turned out that it did not. My savings went dry and my hope in something better began to fade. I was coasting on emotional fumes. With every rejected resume, every failed plan, and every attempt to dig my way out of this mess, nothing changed. The message I kept hearing was wait. Hold on a bit longer. In the devotion "The Isolation Chamber," Os Hillman describes the place of waiting as:

*There is a time and place in our walk with God in which He sets us in a place of waiting. It is a place in which all past experiences are of no value. It is a time of such stillness that it can disturb the most faithful if we do not understand that He is the one who has brought us to this place for only a season. It is as if God has placed a wall around us. No new opportunities--simply inactivity.*

When Moses led the Israelites out of Egypt, he led them to the Red Sea. The Egyptians were closing in behind them and it seemed as if there was no way out. They were trapped. They were terrified and cried out to God, "Was it because there were no graves in Egypt that you brought us to the desert to die? It would have been better for us to serve the Egyptians than to die in the desert!" (Exodus 14:11-12).

No one likes waiting, and during these times of "stalemate" we begin to question God. We begin to unravel and crave those old and familiar places. Like the Israelites, we start craving the fish, the onions, and the leeks. We want the "positions" of comfort and what is secure.

We can complain or we can see the position for what it really is—a desert place. In the devotion "Desert Training," Os Hillman describes the desert place as:

*The desert holds a special place in God's Word. The Scriptures portray the desert as a place of inspiration and exaltation—a place where people met God in a powerful new way. For Joseph, a deep pit in the desert was the first stop on a 13-year journey through desolation and despair. That 13-year desert experience served to break Joseph's self-will and self-confidence. It taught him that he could not control anything and that he needed to rely on God to manage the events in his life. Joseph's desert trial prepared him by scorching the youthful pride and arrogance out of his young life so that when he was 30 years old he could rule Egypt at Pharaoh's side in a spirit of humility and servanthood.*

This time of waiting in my life symbolized a monumental shift in control of the game. I left the position of defeat and began heading to a position of trust. For the first time, I was opening up space so God could be in control. Lack of trust was/is my greatest stumbling block. I desperately needed to trust the plan God has for my life and sit out on the sidelines for a while. The game was far from over. It was actually just beginning.

If you find yourself in a stalemate position or a time of inactivity, I understand how difficult this position may be, especially if you are a mover like me. Set out for a while. Get some rest, so you can get your head back in the game. Your place of promise is on the horizon, and you are exactly where you need to be.

*Your journey has molded you for your greater good, and it was exactly what it needed to be. Don't think that you've lost time. It took each and every situation you have encountered to bring you to the now. And now is right on time.*—Asha Tyson

# 15 THE POSITION OF TRUTH

*A game is like a mirror that allows you to look at yourself.*—Robert Kiyosaki

Time went on and my body began to heal. I filled most of my days talking and emailing my good friend Jeff. Jeff and I met in college and became great friends. His job was suffering due to the sluggish economy, and he had some free

time on his hands as well.

He became my accountability partner, and I became his. We created a safe place emotionally where I could trust him and he could trust me. Over email, we shared the good, the bad, and the ugly. I shared every intimate detail of my time teaching and he shared his thoughts and feelings about his relationship at the time. At first I was ashamed. I was embarrassed to tell him the things I had done. However, he did not cast judgment, only love and grace. I'll never forget his words that changed the course of my thinking during this time.

*We all have days we are not at our best. I'm the "KING" of not my best. If not for the day of not "my best" your journey may not be on the right path now and the lives you touch and influence would not be as significant as they are. God has a plan for you and spending it in that particular classroom was not the ultimate plan but just one small part of it. Or was it small?*—Jeff

His words were medicine to my soul and fit exactly into the empty place of my heart. He helped me realize how this experience fit into my puzzle and my purpose. This new revelation would be the turning point in my direction of travel and help me accept the truth about myself and most importantly, forgive myself.

*In the quiet, the truth emerges.*—Wayne Muller

I hate taking medicine in any form. I gag at the thought of it actually. My grandmother always had to crush up my medicine in a spoon full of juice for me to get it down. That's how I feel about the truth. I hate to swallow it.

During my time of unemployment, I also spent a great deal of my time with my friend Angie and her three-year-old son Asher. One night we decided to make Christmas cookies as I was dying to use my *Christmas Story* leg-lamp cookie cutter. We were preparing the batter, when Asher flipped on the switch to the mixer. Flour went flying everywhere, and we found ourselves covered in a thin film of white dust.

After we cleaned up our mess and baked our cookies, I helped Angie get Asher ready for bed. He had been sick so he had to take his medicine. As soon as Angie approached him with the medicine, he responded with kicking and screaming. I don't blame him. Of course, I had to play the bad guy and hold him down. I felt bad for doing so. We eventually got his medicine down and I eventually accepted the truth about my teaching incident.

*Opposition is like a mirror and reveals what is inside us.*—Unknown

During my time in encampment, I had ample time to evaluate the previous course of events. The incident at school forced me to turn the mirror inward, and I got a glimpse of the strongholds still controlling my life. These unfortunate circumstances revealed the masks I had worn all my life. I was not invincible and could not do everything on my own. I had to let go of my need for control, and I needed to ask others for help.

God has spent many years giving me medicine in the form of closed doors, terminated relationships, heartaches, jobs not received, jobs not renewed, and most importantly humility. As I kicked and screamed and did everything in my power to resist, He held on. He knew how much stronger I would be for the medicine. I am sure He felt bad for playing the "bad guy" just like I did with my little friend Asher. If I was going to be free of worry, stress, anxiety, and the constant need for control, I was going to have to swallow the truth.

*Get the inside right. The outside will fall into place.*—Eckhart Tolle

In the winter of 2009, western Kentucky and north-west Tennessee were hit with a paralyzing ice storm. The storm left the area immovable for several weeks. The ice that blanketed the trees was so heavy that it took down power lines. My cousin Shelly wrote of these unforgettable events on January 27, 2009, in her blog titled *Icy Day.*

*Well, today the ice is heavy and there are many in my city without power. Please pray that we don't have more power outages. We are supposed to get 1–3 inches of snow on top of the ice later and that in and of itself could cause more outages.*

*The ice on the trees is beautiful, as if they are made of glass. A simple thing like ice can make these large creations fragile in just a matter of hours. There are trees down everywhere across Hopkinsville and my son said upon return from his Dad's in the country that you could stand outside and just hear all the trees in the woods popping as limbs succumbed to ice.*

*Sometimes our lives are like that . . . we are rock solid, feel like we are an example of what life should be. Then a storm comes and sticks to us so fast and so hard that we begin to break into pieces and start falling apart. We had no idea that even those who are strong are sometimes no match for a storm.*

*At times like this, we need to put God first, and let him help us pick up the pieces that are broken. Give it all to Him and He can fix what the storm has broken. We will be more beautiful in His eyes because sometimes the storm prunes things away that didn't need to be there in the first place, we just thought that they were integral to our lives, but God knows best.*

In reading this, I realized that I needed to allow God to put me back together. Before He could put the pieces back together, I had to accept the truth about myself and forgive myself. In order to do this, I began blogging myself. I was not that great at first. I merely just threw thoughts onto a virtual page. Over the course of time, I began to grow as a writer, and my writing found its purpose. I began to open up and share more intimate details of my life, which in turned helped others.

As I began revisiting the painful chapters of my life, I began to realize they were important too. They helped to form the woman I am becoming. However, those painful chapters are not the end of the story. Donald Miller said that there is a writer outside ourselves plotting a better story for us, interacting with us even, and whispering a better story into our consciousness. I needed to tell those hard parts of the story and finally make peace with them. I needed to find a better story.

When I first set out to write and share my story, I had no working knowledge of writing and publishing a book. I didn't even know where to begin. I had a manuscript and a theme for my book, or at least I thought I did.

I randomly read where first-time author, Annie Downs, had self-published her book through WestBow Press, a division of Thomas Nelson. She made it sound so simple. I checked out their website and discovered they were hosting the 2010 Women of Faith writing contest.

The grand prize winner would receive, at the sole discretion of Thomas Nelson, an opportunity to have her book sold and carried under the Women of Faith name. If Thomas Nelson exercised their right not to publish, then the winner would receive a free self-publishing package from WestBow.

I jumped at the chance and threw my hat in along with 749 other eager women pursuing a dream to have their life in big fine print. Keep in mind, the concept of chess to illustrate my story had not been conceived at this point.

As any aspiring author, I had dreams, dreams of reaching millions of readers and being on the New York Times Best Seller's list. I cruised through the aisles of Lifeway Christian Bookstore and Barnes and Noble, envisioning the exact spot on the shelf where my book would sit. When I passed the mark-down section, I prayed for God to spare me of this. *Please don't make me a mark-down. Please.*

When the crushing news arrived a few months later that I did not even make the top 30 finalists, I was devastated. What was wrong with my book? Was my book boring? Did it not have enough details? Did it have too many details?

One random afternoon while walking with a friend, I

shared my disappointment in which she shared her heart about why she thought the book was going nowhere. She said the words I will never forget, "Yes, you have a story to tell, but you are going about it the wrong way. People with our past don't want to relive it again in details of another. They want to read about your story, but in not too much detail."

The very next day Beth Moore, one of my favorite Bible teachers and authors, confirmed those exact words in words of her own on the blog post *My Favorite Fill in the Blank*.

*Some whole stories don't need to be told in public but they do indeed need to be redeemed. To me, the line is drawn where the glory to God and the good to the listeners profoundly exceed the pain of the testimony. If the listener will likely be left with graphic visuals and oppressive thoughts or pervasive sadness, we need to refrain from telling it in detail. In those occasions, generalities are best. We don't have to tell people everything to tell them an important something.*

Like Beth and my friend said, I have something to tell, I just don't need to provide all the painful details. It's like collecting magnets. I love collecting them. My fridge tells a story of great adventure and all the places I have traveled to—California, South Carolina, New York, Florida, and even Jamaica. In each chapter of my story, I just need to provide a little snapshot of the story just as the magnet captures a visual of where I traveled. Hopefully, the reader will get the "picture" and not have to travel back to the painful memory lane.

I took my friends' advice and kept on writing. I kept revising until I found my concept and the story I wanted to tell. Knowing what I know now, this book wasn't supposed to be published then. There were more chapters to write and more stories to live out. This book had to find its purpose — the game of life.

If I could encourage you with one thing, I would say: don't run away from your story, embrace it. Embrace all the parts—the good, the bad, and the ugly. Keep telling your story and revise when needed. Accept the truth about yourself and forgive yourself too. The world is looking for individuals who have made mistakes, but have not let those mistakes define them.

The world is looking for great storytellers. Those who take risks and bear it all. The world is looking for hope and encouragement, and your very story could be what the world is looking for.

*Owning our story and loving ourselves through the process is the bravest thing we will ever do.*—-Brene Brown

# PHASE THREE: THE END GAME:

*Hunt Down the King*

# 16 THE POSITION OF PROMOTION

*Most people give up just when they're about to achieve success. They quit on the one yard line. They give up at the last minute of the game one foot from a winning touchdown.*—Ross Perot

The end game is the closing stage of the game. It is difficult to define when you transition from the middle phase

to the end phase. However, a visible sign may be the few pieces remaining on the board, and the fact that the king is found in the center of the board and ready to attack your pieces. This is the time where you have made all your game-playing strategies, and your purpose is in full view—hunting down the king.

One way of hunting down the king is to promote the pawn. A pawn that cannot be blocked or captured by enemy pawns on its way to be promoted is called a passed pawn. A pawn that advances to its eighth rank or all the way to the opponent's side of the board is promoted. The pawn can be promoted to another piece of the same color, with exception of the king, and it immediately takes its new position on the board.

It is most common for a pawn to be promoted to the queen and that is referred to as "queening." If another piece is chosen, that is called "under promotion." Under promotion is considered when a promotion to a queen would give an instant stalemate (a place where a piece cannot move). The pawn is only worth one point. If the pawn can be promoted, its value increases, causing you to gain material advantage, and the better the material advantage, the more pieces to attack with.

*The grandmaster can use a single pawn to checkmate the enemy's plans.*—Mark Batterson

In the game of life, we have opportunities for advancement and second chances. Every day offers a chance for a second chance, even a third, fourth or fifth. God is ready to give you a fresh start. We have to be willing to hand over the parts of our lives that are messy and broken and forgive ourselves.

Moses was given the job of delivering the Ten Commandments to God's people. After 40 days and 40 nights on the mountain with God, Moses descended down from Mt. Sinai and carried with him tablets of God's work—

The Ten Commandments (Exodus 31 - 32). Meanwhile, the Israelites were becoming impatient with Moses. It was taking him too long to come down from the mountain.

They said to Aaron, "Come, make us gods who will go before us. As for this fellow Moses who brought us out of Egypt, we don't know what has happened to him." Aaron complied with their request and took their gold earrings and made them into an idol in the shape of a calf. The Israelites began worshipping their new god. When Moses descended down the mountain, he saw his people worshipping a golden calf, and he was enraged. He smashed the tablets.

*When Moses approached the camp and saw the calf and the dancing, his anger burned and he threw the tablets out of his hands, breaking them to pieces at the foot of the mountain. And he took the calf the people had made and burned it in the fire; then he ground it to powder, scattered it on the water and made the Israelites drink it.*—Exodus 32: 19-20 (NIV)

Those words sent me in a downward spiral to that painful time in my classroom. I was a teacher carrying out God's work, but I let my emotions get the best of me. Out of my frustration, I smashed God's tablets. I thought my dreams were dead and tucked neatly in the grave, but God's actions towards Moses reminded me they were not. God is a God of second chances.

Moses was given another opportunity to deliver the Ten Commandments and the opportunity was captured in Exodus 34:1, and I was given another opportunity to work with children again. This was my chance to wipe the slate clean and begin my career again.

*You can't build an end scene as beautiful as this by sitting on a couch.*—Unknown

In August 2009, life began to bloom again. It was as if the harsh, bitter winter was over and spring had finally sprung. I met my to-be boyfriend Steve, the one who ignores overhead signs on the interstate <insert smiley face>. We ran in a mutual circle of friends and randomly met one night at a friend's birthday party. Our chance meeting was electric, and it was just the spark I needed to revive my lifeless heart.

Then a few months later in November, I landed an after-school tutoring job working about 12 hours a week. I started generating a little income, getting out of the house, and feeling as if I was a member of society again. Love was on the horizon, and I was finally moving forward. However, if the enemy ever sees that momentum is building, he will call a timeout to bring the game to a screeching halt, and so he did.

In February 2010, Beth Moore was on Lifeway's book tour promoting *So Long Insecurities*. I loved Beth Moore, and I loved this book. I devoured it, actually. I stood in line, met Beth, and had her sign my copy of the book. I was thoroughly enjoying the day and finally walking with a little spring in my step.

After I finished tutoring later in the day, I was headed home around 4:45 p.m. when I noticed I had three missed calls from an unknown number. Before I could return the call, I got a text from my next-door neighbor Justin saying something was wrong at my house and to call immediately. When I got him on the phone, he apologetically told me that someone broke into my house. His wife, Tonya, not knowing at the time, had stumbled across the break in. She was the one trying to call me.

Tonya had been walking her dog after work and came across a young woman sitting in the car talking on her cell phone. She overheard the woman say, "There is someone at the front door." The woman quickly hung up the phone and told Tonya that she and her boyfriend were looking at houses for sale.

Tonya found their activity suspicious as there were no houses for sale in the surrounding units. She quickly walked to her house to secure it and to call the police. By the time the police got down to my place, the two intruders (the woman in the car and the man in my house) had bailed.

Frantically, hanging up the phone with Justin, I called my other neighbor and friend Meri and asked her if she could wait at my place until I got home. I peeled out of the parking lot at the school and raced home. I could not get home quick enough. I hit every red light possible. I whipped into my parking space and actually just about hit the car of the policeman who was there surveying the damage.

When I walked into my house, I burst into tears. *Why would someone do this? Why me?* Then panic set in. *My cats! Where were my cats?* They are scared of everything. They run at the sound of a doorbell. *Did they run out the door during all the chaos? What happened to them?* Hours later I found them wedged under my dresser.

The police determined that the intruder hopped over my privacy fence and busted down the back door with a crowbar to get inside. From what I could tell of the damage inside, my laptop and Wii were the only two possessions taken. The enemy knew what he was doing. I barely made enough money to make ends meet. *How on earth would I pay for a new door and replace all that was stolen?*

Sure, possessions can be replaced, but my security could not. I felt so violated. Someone uninvited entered into my home and plumaged through my personal things. This feeling was hard to overcome. I was on edge, worried, and fearful that the intruders might come back. It took months before I felt safe and actually got a good night's rest.

My insurance company replaced what was stolen, and I got my back door repaired. Time went on and eventually I was able to sleep again. Life resumed once again. Shortly thereafter my luck would change again. I landed a contracting position as an assessment editor for a publishing firm. We created summative and diagnostic tests for various school districts across the country. During my time there, I truly fell in love with writing and publishing. I began to emerge as a writer. I began to build my confidence and credibility again.

*From my earliest youth, my enemies have persecuted me, but they have been unable to finish me off.*—Psalm 129:2–4

In the game of chess, we can hunt down the king by promoting the pawn to a queen, and we have that opportunity in life too. We have every opportunity to leave the victim mentality behind and become a victor.

Esther is a character in the Bible who was an orphan and found herself promoted to a Queen. When Esther was just a young girl, she found herself as an orphan after her parents had died. Her cousin, Mordecai adopted and raised her. When King Xerxes was in search of a new queen, he chose Esther.

The king fell in love with Esther and he was far more in love with her than with any of his other women or any of the other virgins—he was totally smitten by her. He placed a royal crown on her head and made her queen in place of Vashti (Esther 2:17).

Haman, a powerful man in their kingdom, hated the Jews and plotted to have them killed. Mordecai convinced Esther to speak to the king and plead for the lives of the Jewish people. Her brave actions ended up saving her people. Serena Woods, author of *Grace Is for Sinners*, spoke of Esther in this way:

> *God knew what He was doing with Esther and she made it easier by not trying to stay in her comfort zone. She didn't know why these things were happening with her, but when the call finally came, she was in the perfect position. He had been positioning her the whole time. He had been training her and preparing her with the tools of her everyday struggles and spaces.*

God spent most of Esther's life leading her out of her comfort zone so when she became Queen, she would be in the perfect position to save the lives of her people. We may never obtain the title of Queen, but once we decide to be a victor and not a victim, we are promoted. By changing our mindset, we place ourselves in that perfect position so we can begin taking back everything that was stolen from us.

In I Samuel 30, the story is told of David and his desire to take everything back that his enemy had taken prisoner. The Amalekites had raided David and his men's camp, leaving nothing untouched. They captured the women, the children, the sheep, the cattle, and when that was not enough, they burned the camp to the ground.

Imagine returning to your camp and everything, absolutely *everything* is gone. How devastating must it feel to see that? To know that everything you loved and everything you worked for was gone in an instant. David could have easily accepted defeat, but the loss fueled David's determination to capture the king and take everything back.

The Lord told David, "Yes, go after them. You will surely recover everything that was taken from you." David pursued the Amalekites just as God instructed and he got back absolutely everything taken from him.

Pastor Denny Livingston said you have to fight for what was stolen—your marriage, your kids, your faith, your childhood, or your dignity. The enemy is not going to freely hand over what he took from you. He took it for a reason. You have to determine that every day you are going to fight with everything you have. It is our God-given right to be restored (Joel 2:25), to be redeemed, and to receive a double portion for our pain (Isaiah 61:7-11). We have the right to fight for what was taken.

Every day that I get out of bed, I fight for the childhood that was stolen. This journey to take back what was stolen has lasted a lifetime. For most of my adult life, I sought professional-based counseling, faith-based counseling, and completed countless Bible studies, *Breaking Free*, *Believing God*, and *Life Interrupted*, just to name a few, in order to provide relief, seek comfort and make some sense of all the pain and anguish. I've read God's word countless times. I attend church regularly. I sat under various preachers—some good and some not so good.

I have worked through every gamut of emotions I have ever felt—anger, resentment, bitterness, sadness, and depression. I have walked through forgiveness of my parents, my grandparents, and myself. I have read every book that Joyce Meyer has published, like *Battlefield of the Mind*, *Anxious for nothing*, and *Managing Your Emotions*. I have listened to countless hours of Joyce's teachings on audio CDs. I have watched so many shows, programs, and read so many books by Beth and Joyce that I feel as if I really know them. We are close friends due to the journey we shared together. Shelly would fall out on the floor laughing upon me saying, "Well, Beth told me to do that. Joyce told me to do this." I am sure I seemed crazy, but you've got to be a little mad and irrational if you want to dig yourself out of the pits of hell.

These books that I speak of and these authors that I quote throughout the book are like players in my game. They pick me up when I am down and hopeless. They give me inspiration to get back up again. They are like extra pieces of defense.

Looking at my personal library display horrifies me. It's like opening the vault to my damaged soul. *Nichole is broken. Nichole is insecure. Nichole has landed in the pit a time or two. Nichole needs to learn to live beyond her feelings.*

Yes, I have been everything I have just described. I have this vast collection of books and audio CDs because I was so hungry for change. I wanted peace. I wanted to be whole. I wanted to be restored. The key to change is to accept what you see standing in the mirror, dig through the truth, and keep going through until you reach the other side of healing.

Healing will not take place overnight. In borrowing the words from Tracie Miles and a slight modification, shame, disgrace, and worthlessness run deep into a person's spirit. It takes a lot of digging, God's mercy, and a lot of time for God to unearth the deeply rooted damage hidden in the caverns of the soul.

*Please deliver us from everything, but Your glory.*—Beth Moore

My niece Madison is eight years old and is in the third grade. She is beautiful (a perfect blend of her mom and dad), she is loud, she is funny, and she is sassy. She loves to play outdoors, ride the family go-cart, or go hunting with her dad. She's more of a tomboy, but still has diva flair.

She will climb in your lap and poke her fingers up your nose and in your ears. She will ask you direct questions like, "Aunt Nichole, does your bangs bother you falling in your face?" Then she will cover your face with kisses and hop off your lap and take off running into her next adventure. I'm mean seriously? Do my bangs hang in my face? I thought my hair was stylish.

Madison and I, Christmas 2012

What is most appealing about Madison is her innocence. Her heart is as big as the ocean, and she loves like no other. I love that the world has not tainted her yet. I love that she loves with no boundaries and asks those questions that drive you to the truth and make you realize you need a new hairstyle <insert smiley face>.

I was once like Madison: full of zeal and a budding new life. I had a bit of sassiness in me as well. I was often found blocking the television, with my hairbrush microphone in hand, performing songs like *Just a Swinging* by John Anderson. It was my dream to be a Solid Gold Dancer and dance to the top ten hits of the week.

Outside my apartment, age 5

My cousin Sam and I "riding" the horse outside of the grocery store.

I was a child who simply wanted to be a child, but that's not how the cards played out for me. My first moves were manipulated by someone who wanted to hurt me and ultimately destroy me and my little spirit got crushed along the way.

The beauty of this all is that it's not over yet. My childhood will not be a complete loss. I can recover all the innocence that was lost. I can get my promotion. Kelly Minter, author of *The Fitting Room*, describes promotion as:

> *Could it really be that God is gathering all the years of wrongdoing to your soul, harvesting it for an unimaginable feast He is preparing, and spreading it on a table He is setting? And not just for heaven, but for some very tangible realities here on earth? Just a thought; or more accurately, a truth for those who are willing to trust their souls to a faithful Creator.*

What if God is taking all of our experiences, all of our hardships, and all of our defeats and gathering them up for a Divine purpose? What if He is setting us up for something that is bigger than us and something we cannot quite conceive?

Life is too short and I don't want to settle for an under promotion, and I don't want to miss out on this unimaginable feast that Kelly Minter described. It would be a disgrace to the purpose I was created for, after all.

I want it all: the dreams—to publish books and travel across the country sharing my story, the promotions, a husband and children, health, and happiness. I want to be promoted like Esther. I may never save a nation from genocide, but I can only hope that one day I will be promoted to a position of great influence that will positively impact people to never give up and to live out a better story.

Do you believe that you can be promoted? Do you believe that you can be used for some purpose bigger than yourself? Do you want to recover everything that you lost? Do you want to reclaim your marriage, your health, your innocence? If you do, you have to be tenacious. You have to be determined to fight no matter the cost. Stay in the game, fight for what you believe and what you have lost. Go after everything and get that promotion!

*Life sometimes offers us a second chance to right our wrongs. Those second chances often come disguised as tragedy waiting to be recognized as a miracle.*—Kathleen Gage

# 17 CHECKMATE—THE POSITION OF SURRENDER

*No one ever won a chess game by betting on each move. Sometimes you have to move backward to get a step forward.*—Amar Gopal Bose

All games must start, all games must finish, and a winner must be declared. In chess, declaring a winner is called checkmate: the time when the opponent's king is threatened

by the opponent's pieces and the king has no possible moves to make, but to surrender.

When I think of the end of a game, the word "closure" immediately comes to mind. I want a satisfying ending to the game. In some way, I have been grasping for closure to my childhood, dissolved relationships, and my teaching career. I am missing my satisfying ending, and I am determined to get it.

In May 2011, after sitting out on the sidelines of my faith, I reluctantly stepped back into the doors of a church, Point of Mercy. I was going to church previously, my old church actually, but I was just taking space up on the pew. I was not really pursuing a relationship with God. My cousin, Shelly, started attending Point of Mercy around 2010 and was begging me to start attending.

I was a bit gun-shy considering all that had happened before at our previous church in Clarksville, Tennessee. After months of resisting the urge to go, I finally gave in. Walking through the doors of Point of Mercy frightened me. My hands were clammy, my heart was pounding, and I found it hard to breathe. I feared the potential risk of getting hurt from believing in something, believing in something I could not see. I was not ready to put my heart or myself back out there.

As I sat in the pew, listening to Pastor Bobby McCool preach his message titled "The Art of Positioning," the tears began to flow, and God's peace completely washed over me. I knew I was exactly where I needed to be. I was at home.

Over the course of two years, I worked through every heartache, every experience, and every failure. I opened myself up to God so He could heal me. During this time of transition, my two-year relationship with Steve dissolved. God started challenging me about the status of our relationship, the fact that we were not married.

When I felt the need to establish some boundaries in our relationship, since Steve was not ready to get married, we started drifting apart. His relationship with God was not at the same level of mine, and he did not share my convictions.

I had plans of marrying him. I had a wedding book, a five-inch blue binder with all the details planned waiting to come to life: the colors, the dress, the ring, and the happily ever after. Our relationship did not end because we did not love each other; it was because we wanted different things. I wanted the commitment. I wanted to be married, but he was not ready. He was content and was in no hurry to move to the next level in our relationship.

I began to pull away because I was eaten up with guilt. We were in an intimate relationship and it felt wrong, especially since we were not married. Maybe he felt as if he were being backed into a corner, I am not sure. Instead of moving forward, he checked out. Our relationship was over in an instant. No dramatic ending, just two people separating because the values were different. I was heartbroken.

It was extremely hard for me to let him go. He is was/is a great man. He saved me from the pit of despair, and he brought me back to life. I prayed fervently for this relationship. The connection was instant, and the chemistry was undeniable. He was sensitive, attractive, passionate, driven, and funny. His embrace was strong, and I felt safe inside. I began to trust again because of him.

Not only did my relationship end with Steve, my contract work as an assessment editor ended too. The work was over and on December 30, 2011, I found myself unemployed again with little to no warning. For the first few weeks, I threw myself a little pity party comprised of eating chips and guacamole and watching episodes of *Live with Kelly* and *The Young and the Restless*.

I continued this way of living until my friend Angie dragged me out of my rut. Angie was a stay-at-home mom, or I should say an on-the-go, non-stop mom of my little friend Asher (the one I baked cookies with). She would call and invite me to run to Costco or just to hang out at her house. I was bored, broke, and up for just about anything that got me out of my condo. I was over the "camping" phase of life.

Besides, she had cable. I never realized there were so many channels. My TV line up consisted of 2 to12 stations or whatever my little rabbit ears could produce. Not only did she have lots of shows to watch, she had lots of dirty dishes piled in the sink. *She is probably going to kill me for this one.* I never imagined that a family of three could dirty up so many dishes in a day.

To earn my keep, I helped her clean the house and keep up with Asher. In return, she loved me, fed me, and sent me home with an occasional bottle of wine. Her husband Lee would often joke that he had two wives. We were like sister-wives only I was the cooler wife who did not nag her husband. *Now she really will kill me.*

It was through my evolving friendship with Angie that I learned I had a voice. Angie was brash and her words were abrasive. She would freely say whatever came to her mind and often forgot to turn on her filter. I, on the other hand, was non-confrontational. I had something to say, but I did not have the courage to speak up. Standing in the book section at Costco, I finally decided to push back.

Angie and I were talking about the unexpected rut I found myself in. She was concerned that I was not getting over my heartbreak and that I was depressed. I cannot remember the conversation exactly, but I know I had reached my limit. Instead of nodding my head in agreement, I asked her to give me space to just be and that while I appreciated her concern, she was not an expert on my situation.

Instead of snapping back, Angie just laughed it off and said, "OK," as if it didn't even faze her and we continued on shopping. From that point on, I freely shared my thoughts regardless of how they were received. I also gave myself the freedom to feel my sadness, my anger, and my disappointment in the time frame that I needed. I gave myself grace to just be.

In September 2011, Emily Freeman wrote a book titled *Grace for the Good Girl.* This book fell into my lap at exactly the right time. Emily's words penetrated right to my damaged soul, into the very wounds I still carried with me. I dove into the book and devoured every page. I was so hungry for the truth. Her words reflected an image of me that I had never seen before.

I was hiding behind my masks, masks of being capable, strong, and resilient, but on the inside I was a mess. Emily explained that the "good girl" needed two rescues: one from her Savior and one from herself.

*The good girl does not understand the depth and breadth and height and width of this Lover who came for her, and so this rescue seems inadequate. She lives on the forgiveness side of the Cross, and then begins to work to earn the life. And so she needs a new rescue. This time, she needs to be rescued from herself.*

Emily's words provided the answer that I was looking for. Yes, I had been saved, but not saved from myself and all my self-effort. Out of guilt, I was constantly paying a price to be accepted and loved. I waited the majority of my life for "someone" to recognize me and all that I had to endure. Out of fear of exposure to what lay beneath, I never allowed a complete surrender. I was always torn between wanting to be rescued and protecting the little girl I vowed to protect.

Finally, after 36 years of running and fighting to maintain complete control, I surrendered. I stopped running from God and let Him take over the reins. It seemed I was in need of a rescue from myself, just as Emily had described.

For the next two years, God carefully cut open the wound of my heart and began to pour his love into me (Philippians 1:6). Every time God spoke, I cried. I cried at almost every service at church. I cried while watching random shows on TV. I cried over songs. I cried in the kitchen. I cried in the bathroom. Long gone were the days of always having to be triumphant and pretending that everything was fine. I became unglued.

On a particular Wednesday night service at church in August 2012, in a few short words, Pastor Denny Livingston said something so profound, and through him, the Lord spoke directly to me. Pastor went into great detail about all the hell some of us had faced.

Through his words, God recognized and publicly acknowledged the heartache and the loss I had felt most of my life. It was the acknowledgment I had been waiting for and needed so desperately. At first, I was embarrassed, but then I felt relieved. I felt completely different almost as if the pain never existed. In that instant, it was as if God had placed that final piece that was missing from me having a mended heart. My wound was sutured up. I felt complete, I felt whole, and I felt redeemed.

*As I unravel before God, I'm reminded that He uses what sometimes feels to us like a tangled mess to weave a beautiful tapestry: the story of our lives. This year He wants me to tell this hard chapter in my story, to wrestle with it again and perhaps finally find peace in the mystery.*—Sadee Schilling

In high school at the close of every school year, my dance company presents their annual recital for the proud parents and any willing participant from the public who dared to attend. Not only did we have a recital to showcase our hard work throughout the year, we also put on a special performance through the production Turn Out. We performed *Cats* and *An American Tale*, to name just a few.

The Alhambra Theater, aging in years, sits on the corner near the downtown square. The inside matches the wear and tear of the outside. The wallpaper is ragged, the air reeks of must, and the carpet, burgundy in color, is worn down in spots. The wooden floor of the stage creaks with every step. The lights starring into the stage are bright leaving the audience barely visible. You very much feel alone, but so alive at the same time.

When I was a junior in high school, our dance company Turn Out put on an adaptation of the musical *The Wiz* by Ken Harper. We followed the script to a degree but put a slight twist on the story. I was cast in the role of Evillene, the wicked witch of the West. Here is a snippet from the program.

*Act 2 Scene 1 begins with Dorothy and her trio of friends anxiously making their way to the Land of Oz, along with some extra baggage, who are just along for the trip. It seems something is going on up ahead. It's that evil witch Evillene and her slaves, the Winkies. She's two times as mean as her sister, Evvamene, who ruled in the East. I wonder if there's any way to get rid of her.*

In the movie *The Wiz,* Evillene was flushed down the toilet as a means to get rid of her. She sat high on her porcelain throne until the Winkies flushed her down. As one may assume, I did not die by being flushed down a toilet. The Winkies got rid of me by different means. I was tricked into thinking I was being handed a delicious and satisfying peanut butter and jelly sandwich, only it was poisonous and led me to defeat. To this day, I find it hard to "choke" down a good PB&J <insert smiley face>.

*You had the power all along, my dear.*—Glinda, the Good Witch

Although those days of playing the evil witch are long behind me, I still find myself playing the role of the enemy who must be defeated. I screech, "I'm melting, melting," only this time it is the frigid lining that surrounds my heart that dies, not me. Every kind word, "you are beautiful," "you are brilliant," and "you are inspiring," unleashes belief that in turns melts away the layers a little at a time. With every word I *swallow,* the wound of "you don't matter," or "you won't amount to anything" dies a little bit more, till eventually there is no more.

Who would have thought that something good would triumph over darkness like the Wicked Witch declared? Who would have ever imagined that a sweet little girl from Kansas could be ripped away from everything familiar, everything that comforts her, to pursue a yellow-bricked road to find her true destiny? In the end, she comes to the realization that there really is no place like home.

It happens, and not just on the big screen. It happens in real life too. A sweet, innocent girl from Kentucky, ripped away from her childhood into a violent, dark world, follows a path to find freedom, wholeness, and restoration. While I have never received an Oscar for such efforts, I've played the greatest role in my life.

To find that little girl again and get her back on the path of her true destiny, to overcome darkness with love—that is my greatest feat. She is sassy, she is spunky, and her heart is as big as the ocean. She is beautiful, she is strong, and she certainly has what it takes to defeat an opponent once and for all.

*Checkmate*

At last, the final move has been made, and the enemy has been checkmated. For me, I was my own enemy all along. I let fear and the need for control rule my life. Fear interfered with my happiness, my peace, and my fulfillment.

We all have "demons" that we battle on a daily basis. Sure, the Devil used every form of weapon to attack me. I was robbed of my innocence, my car was broken into, my car was stolen, and my house was broken into. I've had friendships end due to people's loyalties with others, and I've had precious relationships end. However, the Devil couldn't quite defeat me in the end.

Just like a survivor, I have outwitted, outlasted, and outplayed the enemy in both myself and my adversary. I can now step into my place of promise. The journey has been long. The journey has been grueling, but it has so been worth it.

Do you still find yourself unable to defeat your enemy? Do you have real enemies or do you find yourself like me, being your own worst enemy? Maybe it's time to face your "demons," back that king into the corner, and call out "checkmate."

*Until your knees finally hit the floor, you're just playing at life, and on some level, you're scared because you know you're just playing. The moment of surrender is not when life is over. It's when it begins.—* Marianne Williams

# 18 THE POSITION OF PROMISE

*It's hard to be a person who never gives up.*—Babe Ruth

When the Israelites reached the Promised Land, they had to cross over the Jordan River. Before the Israelites could cross over the Jordan River, Joshua sent two spies to look over the land. The land was inhabited by seven Canaanite tribes who were corrupt.

The Israelites requested that they leave peacefully, but the tribes did not, and their actions led to the Battle of Jericho. The Israelites would have to win this battle to take over the Promised Land.

The Battle of Jericho was the first battle of the Israelites during their conquest of Canaan. God spoke to Joshua and told him to march around the city once every day for six days and on the seventh day, they were to march around the city seven times blowing their trumpets. Joshua did as instructed, the walls of the city collapsed, and the Israelites were able to take over the city.

*When there is no enemy within, the enemies outside cannot hurt you.*— African Proverb

Crossing over into the Promised Land did not come easy for the Israelites and it did not come easy for me either. All I knew was a life full of pain. Walking pain free was foreign to me. I immediately wanted to grab my crutches, those vices that kept me up all those painful years. *Wait a minute! You mean there is nothing to fix? I've been healed of that problem? What am I to do now? Where do I go?*

I had a hard time at first. I was so used to the labels of "victim," "broken," "dysfunctional," and "bitter" that I had trouble walking. On many occasions I found myself wanting to turn back and turn to the familiar positions like old habits and relationships. My foot was in one place, but my head was in another.

If I am truly going to get a real grasp of my purpose, then I am going to have to lay my crutches down for good. They no longer have a purpose. True, they have aided my walk to the place I find myself now, but now I am strong enough to stand on my own two feet. I was never meant to live my life entirely with those crutches and neither were you; they were just a means to an end.

*I can't go back to yesterday because I was a different person then.*—
Alice in Wonderland

One of my favorite books and movies is *Eat, Pray, Love*
by Elizabeth Gilbert. Julia Roberts plays Liz in the movie,
which makes for a double bonus. I have loved Julia since she
starred in *Pretty Woman* over 20 years ago. Liz, like me, is on a
journey, a journey to find herself. She comes to the
realization that she is unhappily married and sets off on an
around-the-world one-year journey to rediscover her appetite
for life.

As the title describes, there are three parts to her journey,
like the three phases of chess. Liz begins in Italy where she
has a love affair with food and the Italian language. There she
begins her search for a word, a word to summarize her
journey. Her friends would ask, "Liz, what is your word?"
She would jokingly say, "pizza" and then go eat a whole pie. I
like a woman who goes after what she wants.

Next, she spends a few months in India where she is
stripped of everything and through prayer and meditation she
deals with her past. I totally understand what it feels like to be
"stripped" of everything: job, reputation, credibility, stability,
friends, and comforts. It hurts and it seems as if the process
will never end, but thank God that there is an end.

Liz wraps up her trip with a stay in beautiful Bali where
she finally settles in on her word "Attraversiamo"—which
means "let's cross over." In an unexpected bike accident, she
meets her beloved and handsome Philippe and finally crosses
over into a committed relationship. She lets go of her fears
and her need for control, and she allows herself to love again.

Robin and I, New York City, 2012

Like Liz, I too am on a journey to regain my appetite for life. I can think of no better place to begin this journey than in the Big Apple. In September 2012, my friend Mina and I went to New York City to celebrate our 37th birthdays. My friend Robin, who lives in Connecticut, was able to spend a day with us.

It was my first time visiting New York City and we were blessed with perfect fall-like conditions. Since "idle" is not in my vocabulary, I set out to cover every square mile of Manhattan: Times Square, Broadway, the Financial District, the Statue of Liberty, and the Empire State Building. I'm glad Mina was up for the challenge. We took a big bite out of the apple, and as a result, we could not walk for days.

We saw *Phantom of the Opera* on Broadway. We watched the taping of *Good Morning America* and got a close up of Sam Champion (previous weather man) and George Stephanopoulos (GMA anchor). We took a stroll through Central Park on a crystal clear day. We walked the Brooklyn Bridge. We went to the top of the Empire State Building at midnight. We even tracked down Carrie Bradshaw's (*Sex in the City)* Upper East Side apartment.

We wrapped up the trip with a visit to the Statue of Liberty and the 9/11 Memorial. We took the ferry from Battery Park to first visit the Statue of Liberty. Lady Liberty was undergoing construction, so we could not go inside. The outside said it all. The weather was glorious. The sky was crystal blue with no cloud in sight, which made for a remarkable sight. Lady Liberty stood tall, untouchable, unmoved, yet reflecting freedom for so many.

Mina and I, Statue of Liberty, NYC, 2012

Next, we went to the 9/11 site. Upon entering the site, I was greatly moved, moved to tears and at a loss for words. I was overwhelmed by sadness, yet I sensed peace, inspiration, and hope. The two pools that replaced the north and south tower were beautifully crafted to honor the lives that were lost during the tragic event. The walls surrounding the pools had the names of every life lost etched into them. I could think of no better way to honor so many lives lost.

A short distance away from the pools stands the new Freedom Tower. Two towers destroyed in a horrific act of violence will be replaced by one—one strong tower united in freedom. I love how the tower reflects the city. It casts a perfect image of its surroundings.

This new tower signifies that we can always rebuild. We can always start over. We can always rise from the ashes. Only this time, we are stronger, more secure, and everlasting.

Freedom Tower – 9/11 Memorial September 2012

We all have had a day that we will always remember, and for some of us, it's a day we want to completely erase from the calendar. It's the day that changed our lives completely. One moment, one word, or one action altered our lives completely. We thought we would never recover and that all was lost. Like the scripture says, "Make your memorial, go back to the place where you came from, and remember how you got there (Joshua 4: 5-7)." This book is my memorial. Each chapter reminds me how each position was essential for me to reach my place of promise. I needed them all in order to reach my destination.

*When you turn the construction of your life over to God, He'll build something beautiful.*—Joyce Meyer, *Begin Again*

Throughout King David's journey, he was on a mission to build a temple to honor the Lord. However, he was not able to successfully build the temple until he was victorious over all his enemies (1 Kings 5: 3-5).

Like King David, I am in the process of rebuilding. I am rebuilding my career, my dreams, and relationships. I could not successfully build my temple until my enemies were destroyed, and I made peace with my past. The Lord said, "Afterwards I will return, and I will restore the fallen kingdom of *Nichole* from the ruins. I will rebuild *her*, and I will restore *her*" (Acts 15:16).

*When we put God first, all other things fall into their proper place.—*
Unknown

Right before my trip to the Big Apple, actually April
2012, my former boss at the publishing firm I worked for in
early 2010 called me out of the blue. The company won a
contract to develop an online standardized test for the
Common Core, and they need additional staff. It was the big
break I was waiting for.

I started off as a temporary employee and quickly
advanced to a contractor position. That position did not last
long and a few months later I was offered a full-time position.
It was the first time in over three years that I had a full-time
job.

I was recognized for my contributions to the
development in the pilot phase of the test, and much to my
surprise, I was promoted to co-lead the development of the
math Common Core field test we were building next. The
development consisted of 33,000 items that would be taken
by 4.2 million students in 23 participating states.

This was the first time I would be in a position in this
magnitude and with this much responsibility. I was in front of
customers, and I was making huge decisions, as well as
leading and developing temporary staff. Not only was I in a
highly visible role, I was making connections internally as
well.

The people I encountered and formed friendships with
during those two years were life changing. They were life
family. They kept me sane during that challenging year. We
worked long hours, nights, weekends, and even holidays.
Their prayers, theirs support, and their laughter kept me
moving forward as a leader and together we built a product
we were all extremely proud of.

I also met my friend Rob who challenged me in my
writing and helped me bring my writing to life. Not only did
my writing come to life, I felt as if I did as well. I learned to
speak with confidence, and I learned to believe in myself. I

believe this was where I made true connections to my purpose as author and speaker. When I finally gave into God's plan, I experienced blessings I never imagined. His plans have superseded my own. I assure you, what is waiting for you in the Promised Land is undeniable joy, unexplainable peace, and a rare love never thought possible. I have experienced all that and more, but in order to achieve those things, I had to make up my mind that I would stay the course no matter how difficult the journey would be.

I am here to remind you that you can always rebuild. Once you hand over the rubble to Jesus, the Master Carpenter, he can draft a blueprint of something strong, something beautiful, and something everlasting. He had over 30 years of experience in the area of rebuilding. The new life He built for me has a solid foundation, one that is formed with the truth. You can experience this kind of life. All you have to do is hand over your life to Him. Let Him tear down the structure if is appears to be faulty and unsafe. Let Him build something new.

*We work hard to disown the parts of our lives that were painful, difficult, or sad. But just as we can't rip chapters out of a book and expect the story to still make sense, so we cannot rip chapters out of our past and expect our lives to still make sense. Keep every chapter of your life intact, and keep on turning the pages. Sooner or later you'll understand why every scene, every chapter was needed.*—Sandra Kring

# 19 THE POSITION OF REVELATION

*When the game is over it is really just beginning.*—Jerry Kramer

When the game is over, we are quick to pack up the game and move on to something else. However, in the game of life, the game is never truly over. Life is all about change, and we won't stop changing and growing until the very end of our

life. In an effort to keep growing, we should always take time to evaluate the game we just played. This will help us improve our next game.

In my own evaluation, I considered the following questions: What would I have done differently? Would I have made that move? Would I have passed on that opportunity? Would I have uttered that word? Would I have taken more risks or sat out on the sidelines? How would I have played the game differently, if at all?

Steve Maraboli said, "As I look back on my life, I realize that every time I thought I was being rejected from something good, I was actually being directed to something better." Each position, each advancement, and even each setback was preparing me and lining me up for my overall purpose. Each position was another connection being made, a connecting of the dots, if you will, to fulfill my purpose.

*Realize that everything connects to everything else.*—Leonardo da Vinci

In May 2012, some friends and I went to the Tour de Fat festival in Centennial Park in West Nashville. The Tour de Fat celebrates the invention of the bicycle. The festival starts with a costumed bike parade around Nashville before concluding in the park.

The park was filled with many food trucks, vendors, live music, and outdoor games. Much to my surprise, they had a giant Connect 4 game set up. The game had thick red and black discs to simulate the checkers in the original game. My friend Amanda and I played the best two out of three. She ended up winning. I let her win actually.

Connect 4 - Centennial Park – May 2012

Also, another cool connection to this game was that my one-word resolution for 2012 was "connect." I too, like Liz in *Eat, Pray, Love*, have a word I focus on each year. I chose the word "connect" because I struggle with making my heart connect to what I know in my mind. If I didn't make connections, then I didn't have to feel anything.

By focusing on this word, I was hoping my heart would finally let go and feel everything—even the stuff I spent my life escaping from. I wanted to feel everything possible, I wanted to know everything possible, and I wanted to actually live.

Throughout this whole process of life, I have learned that there are some things I may never understand, like the tragic events of my childhood. The opening line of *My Savior My God* by Aaron Shust pierces my heart every time I hear it. *I am not skilled to understand what God has willed what God has planned. I only know at His right hand stands One who is my Savior.* My eyes begin to flood from the pain of the loss I have dealt with through the course of my life.

I am not skilled to understand sexual abuse of a child, in one instance or in too many times to count. I am not skilled to understand cancer in a young mother who simply wants to be a wife and raise her babies. I am not skilled to understand the man, the father, who walks out on his family to pursue his own desires. I am not skilled to understand why a man has to walk through sickness and cannot find a cure.

I am not skilled to understand loss in any form. I am not skilled to know, because I was not created to know. If I were designed to fully comprehend and accept the pain and the agony that accompanies loss, then there would be no need for a Savior. I was created to fulfill a purpose and to display God's glory. I was given an assignment specifically for me and so are you.

For years, I wrestled with unanswered questions about my abuse. *Why did this have to happen? Why did the abuse last so long?* I was desperate for answers. I thought an answer would bring peace and comfort. A few years back, I finally got the answer I was waiting for, only, it didn't come in the form I was seeking. Beth Moore, my beloved "friend," said something that stopped the questions altogether. She said, "We can give ourselves to purpose. If we cooperate, good will, indeed, come and glory will come to God. Otherwise, He would have forbidden the tragedy."

As hard as this was for me to swallow, there was a purpose for my abuse: to help others and inspire others to overcome. For years, I struggled with hiding my story. I was ashamed. I did not want anyone to know my deep dark secrets. I did not want anyone to know what had happened to me during my childhood. However, I now realize that I would not be who I am today without this painful past and by sharing my story I would find healing.

*Christ never allows the hearts of His own to be shattered without excellent reasons and eternal purposes.*—Unknown

Each day I leave work, I pass the duplex I once lived in about eight years ago. It was actually the place I lived in before I moved to Chicago. It was a charming little two bedroom duplex located on a quiet dead end street and had a 1970s green kitchen, hardwood floors, and lime green tiled bathroom. I loved living there. I loved the convenience of its location. It was close to the mall, restaurants, downtown, and the interstate.

I immediately envisioned my life there: the convenience of that area of town and the ease of a five-minute commute to work. After I got caught up in the moment of what would have been, I began to remember all of the experiences and the friendships that I would have missed out on if I had never moved out of the place.

What about all the wonderful friendships I made, the weddings in Charleston, South Carolina, where the movie *The Notebook* was filmed? What about my spontaneous trip to Mexico and my back-to-back trips to New York City? What about all my experiences in Chicago? They would be nonexistent and my heart would not be as full as it is today.

Sure, I would have also missed all the heartache of a failed career, the ruptured appendix, and unemployment. I would have skipped that season of hardship, but I would have missed out on the joy of knowing God's true heart and finding my true identity.

Throughout my life, I have traveled to many places, some geographically and some emotionally. I have experienced many joyous occasions, and I have had days that I wanted to completely erase. I have experienced both joy and sorrow just like my little poem said.

Through it all, I absolutely know that I would not be the woman I am today without all of those experiences. I know without a shadow of a doubt that without God I would have never made it. He has held my hand throughout this entire experience. He has wiped away my tears. He has replaced my sorrow with joy and peace.

I found an old devotion titled "Preparation for Greatness"

by Os Hillman in my inbox some time ago. The devotion talked about the training ground that God took David through and how it could have been perceived as cruel and unusual punishment. However, it was necessary for what David was to become.

*God was David's source for everything. God gave him the ability to achieve the many extraordinary things in his life. It was a lifelong training ground that moved him from one plateau to another, often dropping into a ravine of despair and hopelessness from time to time. These are God's ways. They drive us deeper and deeper into the heart of Him who has prepared a way for us. Let God take you to the heights or depths He desires for you. He never promised smooth sailing during the trip, but He did promise to be the captain and companion along the way.*

As I stand on the mountain top after leaving the pit of despair and hopelessness, I admire the view and it is absolutely incredible. It is a place that I have never been before. For once, I am healthy, confident, and secure. I am building a life on a foundation that is solid. I now have the ability to achieve extraordinary things in my life.

Many places in my life along the way have felt cruel and undeserved, but they were instrumental in the journey. They were all part of the design of my life and my purpose. Knowing what I know today, I'll gladly go through the depths again to get to the place I am standing today.

If I have learned anything on this journey it's that God keeps His promises. He gave me double for my trouble (Isaiah 61:7). He restored what the locusts ate away (Joel 2:25). He restored me. He gave me undeniable joy, unexplainable peace, and a rare love never thought possible.

He gave me a voice for the voiceless and a passion to help others. I absolutely believe He will do the same for you. Your place of promise is just around the bend. Stay in the game, position yourself to win, and claim your place of promise.

…Stay tuned for my next move.

*I have walked that long road to freedom. I have tried not to falter; I have made missteps along the way. But I have discovered the secret that after climbing a great hill, one only finds that there are many more hills to climb. I have taken a moment here to rest, to steal a view of the glorious vista that surrounds me, to look back on the distance I have come. But I can only rest for a moment, for with freedom come responsibilities, and I dare not linger, for my long walk is not ended.*—Nelson Mandela

*Brokenness doesn't have to be the last chapter of your story.*—Suzie
Eller

# RESOURCES AND HELPFUL INFORMATION

By writing and sharing stories, authors draw us a detailed map on how to make the journey. My road map for making it through my journey of healing and freedom was God's love and pursuit of me, His word, and the wonderful Bible teachers and preachers He placed in my direction. Throughout my journey of healing, those teachers and preachers shared similar experiences and provided information that was instrumental in my recovery.

Joyce Meyer and Beth Moore provided many of the resources in the forms of books, teaching tapes, and Bible studies. Joyce Meyer has a daily program titled *Enjoying Everyday Life*. The program is thirty minutes and provides Biblical teaching on how to enjoy life. She has also written many books. *Battlefield of the Mind* provides ways to win the battle in your mind. If you suffer from worry, doubt, confusion, depression, or anger, this book will help you find peace. *Beauty for Ashes* will help you receive emotional healing from abuse.

Beth Moore concentrates her expertise through Bible studies. *Breaking Free*, both book and Bible study, teaches you how to experience God's peace and His presence by breaking free from strongholds. By reading or participating in the study *Believing God*, you will learn what it means to know and believe in God.

The deeper part of my healing came from reading the workbook *Healing for Damaged Emotions* by David Seamands. I participated in a small-group setting with the direction of a professional counselor. Through the study and God's grace, I uncovered the repressed feelings of my abuse, and through self-discovery, I found healing.

If you are not able to locate a small-group study, then there is a paperback version as well. Seamands also has written *Putting Away Childish Things*. This book requires you to take a closer look at why you react to situations in the way you do.

Although I have not attended, Celebrate Recovery has been highly recommended by several friends. This is a faith-based twelve-step program to provide healing from hurts, hang-ups, and habits. Celebrate Recovery is offered through various churches.

Not only do I give credit to these great teachers and authors, I give thanks to Pastor Denny Livingston. He is the pastor of Point of Mercy in Nashville, Tennessee. He taught me how to pursue God and to never give up on my dreams. His obedience to God in moving to Nashville to restore the church launched my vision of this book. It was during the church's anniversary service that *My Next Move* was birthed.

If you do not know Christ personally or have turned your back to Him, then I invite you to consider or reconsider pursuing a relationship with Him. The benefits are endless. You will experience love, joy, peace, kindness, goodness, faithfulness, gentleness, and self-control (Galatians 5:22). I have included a prayer for forgiving yourself, one for healing, and lastly one to invite Jesus into your life. These prayers changed my life and ultimately saved me.

## Prayer of Forgiveness

Dear Heavenly Father, I understand that there is nothing to gain by holding myself in unforgiveness and there is everything to gain by releasing myself from unforgiveness and beginning the process of healing. I want to move forward and make a positive difference in the future. I confess the ungodly accountability, self-abasement, and the vows I have made to never forgive myself. Because Jesus died for my sins, I choose to forgive myself—to no longer punish myself and be angry with myself. I forgive myself for letting this hurt control me and for hurting others out of my hurt. I repent of this behavior and my attitude. I ask for your forgiveness and healing. God, help me to NEVER again retain unforgiveness of myself or others. Thank you for loving me and for your grace to move forward with you. In Jesus' Name, Amen (AllAboutGod.com)

## Prayer of Healing

God I surrender my life for you to heal me. I ask you for complete restoration and the redemption of all that has been lost in my life. I ask you to bring justice into my life for all the things that have hurt me. If I have hurt someone else, I pray God that you would make that up to them and pay them back for the wrong thing that I have done. Show me if there is something I can do to make it better. But I can only do it through your strength. Father God, I want this healing, but I know that I cannot do this myself. So I ask you today to heal me completely and I will work with you and not give up until the job is completely done. Thank you for all you have done in my life. Thank you for what you are doing right now. And thank you for all that you will do in the future. In Jesus' Name, Amen. (Joyce Meyer Ministries, 2010)

## Prayer of Salvation

Father God I love you. Jesus I believe in you. I need you Jesus. I believe you died on the cross for me. I know that I am a sinner. I am sorry for my sins and I ask you to forgive me. You paid for my sins. Jesus I receive you now into my life and I give myself to you right now. I surrender. I release my life to you. Take me just the way that I am. And now work with me and make me what you want me to be. I believe my sins have been forgiven. I believe I have been saved. I am on my way to heaven and I am going to enjoy the journey. In Jesus' Name, Amen. (Joyce Meyer Ministries, 2010)

# NOTES

Introduction
1.  Miller, Donald. *Scary Close*. Nashville: Thomas Nelson, 2014.
2.  Ryder, Johnny Ray. "The Oak Tree" Web. February 2015.

Chapter 1: The Game of Life
1.  Wikipedia. "The Game of Life" Wikipedia.org. Web. 13 December 2011
    http://en.wikipedia.org/wiki/The_Game_of_Life

Chapter 2: The Game Maker
1.  Romaine, Nancy. "The Father and the Child" Calvary Baptist Church, n.d. Web. November 2010.
    http://calbapchurch.tripod.com/CBCOM/cbcom1.html

Chapter 3: The Design of the Game
1.  Unknown. "Jigsaw Puzzle History" Web. 13 February 2014.
    http://www.ideafinder.com/history/inventions/jigpuzzle.htm
2.  Wikipedia. "Amazing Race". Web. n.d.

http://en.wikipedia.org/wiki/The_Amazing_Race.

3. Rinehart, Paula. *Strong Women Strong Hearts: A Woman's Guide to Cultivating a Wise Heart and Passionate Life.* Nashville: Thomas Nelson, 2001.

Chapter 4: The Object of the Game

1. Wolff, Patrick. *The Complete Idiot's Guide to Chess.* Third Edition. New York: Penguin Group, 2005. Print.

2. Miller, Donald. *A Million Miles in a Thousand Years.* Nashville: Thomas Nelson, 2009.

3. Smallwood, Linda. "Names of God" Myredeemerlives.com. 2000. Web. 16 December 2011.http://www.myredeemerlives.com/namesofgod/yhwh-jehovah.html

Chapter 5: The Players of the Game

1. Wolff, Patrick. *The Complete Idiot's Guide to Chess.* Third Edition. New York: Penguin Group, 2005. Print.

2. Miller, Donald. *A Million Miles in a Thousand Years.* Nashville: Thomas Nelson, 2009.

3. Hillman, Os. "Getting Picked." *TGIF Today God Is First* Volume 2 (2013) no p.

4. *New Living Translation Version.* Bible Gateway. Web. 6 April. 2015.

5. Moore, Beth. *The Beloved Disciple: Following John to the Heart of Jesus.* B&H Books, 2003. Print.

Chapter 6: The Rules of Movement

1. Unknown. "Learn How to Play Chess: The Rules" Chess.com. Web 2011 http://www.chess.com/learn-how-to-play-chess.html

2. Meyers, Joyce. *Beauty for Ashes.* New York: Hachette Book Group, 1994. 57-58.

3. Hillman, Os. "How God Makes Fishermen." *TGIF Today God Is First* Volume 1 (2010) no p. Dated 11.10.2010.

Chapter 7: The Strategies of the Game

1. Unknown. "Checkmate Patterns in Chess" Usefulchess.com. Web. 16 December 2011. http://www.usefulchess.com/tactics/checkmate.htm
2. Chess Teacher. "50 Strategies to Gain the Upper Hand Over Your Opponent" *MyChessblog.com.* Web. 28 March 2009. http://www.mychessblog.com/50-strategies-to-gain-the-upper-hand-over-your-opponent/
3. Collins, Suzanne. *The Hunger Games.* Scholastic, 2008.

Chapter 8: The Starting Position
1. Wheeler, David. "A Beginner's Garden of Chess Openings" Dwheeler.com Web. 2002. http://www.dwheeler.com/chess-openings/
2. Muller, Wayne. *Sabbath – Finding Rest, Renewal, and Delight in our Busy Lives.* New York: Bantam Books, 1999.

Chapter 9: The Position of Preparation
1. Hillman, Os. "Passing the Test." *TGIF Today God Is First* Volume 1 (2013) no p.

Chapter 11: The Blocked Position
1. Pardue, Candice. "The Three Phases of a Chess Game" Justchess.biz. Web. 2004. http://www.justchess.biz/phases2.htm.
2. Hillman, Os. "A Talking Donkey." *TGIF Today God Is First* Volume 1 (2013) no p.

Chapter 14: The Position of Encampment
1. Gerth, Holly. "You're Already Amazing." Grand Rapids: Revell, 2012.
2. Hillman, Os. "The Isolated Chamber." *TGIF Today God Is First* Volume 1 (2010) no p.
3. Hillman, Os. "Desert Training." *TGIF Today God Is First* Volume 2 (2011) no p.

Chapter 15: The Position of Truth
1. Deason, Shelly. "Icy Day" ShellyDeason.com. Web 2014 http://shellydeason.com/2009/01/27/icy-day

2. WestBow Press. "Women of Faith Writing Contest." Web n.d. Westbowpress.com. http://www.westbowpress.com/WomenOfFaith/
3. Moore, Beth. "My Favorite Fill in the Blank." Lproof.org. Web 21 February 2011. http://blog.lproof.org/2011/02/my-favorite-fill-in-the-blank-ever.html

Chapter 16: The Position of Promotion
1. New Living Translation Version. Bible Gateway. Web. 6 April. 2015
2. Wood, Serena "Canvas" Graceisforsinners.com. n.d. Web. http://www.graceisforsinners.com/life/canvas/#ixzz1Xw8curf5
3. Minter, Kelly. The Fitting Room: Putting on the Character of Christ. Colorado Springs: David C Cook, 2011.

Chapter 17: Checkmate—The Position of Surrender
1. Freeman, Emily, P. Grace for the Good Girl: Letting Go of the Try-Hard Life. Grand Rapids: Revell, 2011.

Chapter 18: The Position of Promise
1. New Living Translation Version. Bible Gateway. Web. 6 April. 2015

Chapter 19: The Position of Revelation
1. Hillman, Os. "Preparation for Greatness." TGIF Today God Is First Volume 1 (2010) no p.

Resources and Helpful Information
1. Meyer, Joyce. "Prayer of Healing and Salvation". JoyceMeyer.org. October 2010. Web. http://www.joycemeyer.org/OurMinistries/Broadcast/
2. Unknown. "Forgiving Yourself – Helping Others and Yourself" AllAboutGod.com n.d. Web. 16 October 2009. http://www.allaboutgod.com/forgiving-yourself.htm

# ABOUT THE AUTHOR

Nichole Cornelius is a curriculum writer by day and a dreamer/entrepreneur by night. She is currently building her business, Bookends Media, with hopes of starting her own publishing firm and launching her motivational speaking career. She is currently single and lives in Nashville, Tennessee.